2 04

WE CAN BE BRAVE

MARIANN EDGAR BUDDE

EPISCOPAL BISHOP OF WASHINGTON

WE
CAN BE
BRAVE

HOW WE LEARN TO BE
BRAVE IN LIFE'S DECISIVE MOMENTS

ADAPTED FOR YOUNG READERS BY
BRYAN BLISS

DUTTON CHILDREN'S BOOKS

DUTTON CHILDREN'S BOOKS

An imprint of Penguin Random House LLC
1745 Broadway, New York, NY 10019
penguinrandomhouse.com

Design by Anna Booth
Text set in Garamond Premier Pro

Library of Congress Cataloging-in-Publication Data is available.

Manufactured in the United States of America
BVG

ISBN 9798217113811 (hardcover)
1   3   5   7   9   10   8   6   4   2

ISBN 9798217113828 (paperback)
1   3   5   7   9   10   8   6   4   2

The authorized representative in the EU for product safety and compliance is
Penguin Random House Ireland, Morrison Chambers, 32 Nassau Street,
Dublin D02 YH68, Ireland, https://eu-contact.penguin.ie.

For Amos and Patrick

Watching you grow in grace and courage
remains the greatest blessing of my life.

PREFACE

"Boldness be my friend!"
—William Shakespeare

I believe we first learn what it feels like to be brave when we are young, when nearly every day we must do something that we've never done before. With this belief in mind, I jumped at the chance to publish an edition of my book *How We Learn to Be Brave* for young readers.

Parenting was, for me, a master class in courage—not a class that I taught, but one where I was the student, witnessing the countless times our sons stepped into the unknown, attempted the impossible, made mistakes and learned from them, and persevered toward the horizons only they could see. While I kept our sons' stories mostly in the background of these pages, what I saw in them as they grew, and continue to see in the men they have become, informed every word.

It has never been my intention or desire to be best known for words spoken to or about President Donald J. Trump. I am a bishop in the Episcopal Church, which means that I spend most days doing all I can to support the clergy and congregations in my care, far from the public eye. Yet all Christians have a public role, for we pledge at our baptism "to strive for justice and peace, and to respect the dignity of every human being."

I first wrote *How We Learn to Be Brave* after my response to President Trump holding a Bible for a photo while standing in front of St. John's Lafayette Square reverberated across the world.

This was in June 2020, during the intense days following the murder of George Floyd in Minneapolis by a police officer, which sparked protests across the country. I took issue with the president's misappropriation of sacred symbols—the Bible and the church itself—and with the order to forcibly remove hundreds of peaceful protestors in Lafayette Square Park to clear the way for the president's photo op.

My goal in writing was not to dwell on that one decisive moment, but rather to put it in perspective, by describing the many decisive moments in life that teach us all how to be brave.

Five years later, on January 22, 2025, I gave the sermon at an interfaith prayer service for the nation held at the Washington National Cathedral the day after Donald Trump returned to the White House. It was the global response to that sermon that prompted Dutton Books to propose a young reader's edition and to invite Bryon Bliss to join as co-author.

A bit of background about the sermon and the service itself:

Washington National Cathedral has been the site of an interfaith prayer service on the day after presidential inaugurations since the 1930s. In more recent years, the Cathedral allowed the presidential inaugural committee to plan much of the service, including the selection of a preacher. But in June 2024, the Cathedral announced that it would retain control over all aspects of the service. Its theme would be national unity. After a particularly bruising and divisive campaign season, the Cathedral's goal was to offer prayers for healing, asking God to help unite our country. Regardless of who won, I, as bishop of the Diocese of Washington, would preach.

Thus, my assignment was clear, and I had ample time to prepare. I was to preach about unity to a divided country. But what is unity and how do we achieve it?

As a spiritual leader, I faced a real dilemma: how to speak and pray for unity when, as a nation, we are actively undermining the foundations upon which unity depends. From a political perspective, President Trump and the Republican Party had every reason to assume a mandate for change, having won every branch of the federal government, with a plurality of voting Americans expressing their support for his agenda. During the inauguration ceremonies, President Trump was surrounded by clergy who prayed in thanksgiving that God "saved his life and raised him up with strength and power." In his inaugural address, the president himself declared his belief that in surviving an assassin's bullet during the campaign, he "was saved by God to make America great again." He claimed for himself the mantle of unifier and peacemaker.

In choosing to speak to the necessary foundations of national unity, which include honoring the inherent dignity of every human being, speaking the truth, and humility born of self-awareness, I sought to address, as respectfully as I could, what was not being acknowledged: that millions of people were simply not included in the president's vision of America. I appealed to him to have mercy on those in our country who had every reason to be scared.

The responses to my words were immediate, intense, and reflective of our divisions as Americans. There was no middle ground. Some angrily demanded an apology and called for my resignation, even expulsion from the country. Others expressed effusive gratitude for my courage. Many described the sermon as prophetic, a brave example of speaking truth to power. I didn't feel like a prophet. I felt like a pastor, speaking to the country I love.

In preparing to speak at this prayer service, among the questions I struggled with was how to say what needed to be said. Of course, I wondered what might God have to say to us at this moment, and I sought guidance from our sacred texts. How could I issue a gentle but clear warning that prayers for unity mean nothing if our actions are based in contempt for those who see the world differently? Equally important, how could I humanize those described in sweeping, derogatory generalizations and, with as much calm and respect as I could muster, make a plea for mercy?

While the response it evoked was extraordinary, as sermons go, it was pretty basic fare—an attempt to apply biblical truths to a particular moment, with spiritual themes not unlike those preached every Sunday in churches around the world. The main reason I have chosen to remain in the public eye after January 22, 2025, is to give witness to a way of being Christian that recognizes all human beings as created in the image of God and seeks to follow in Jesus's way of love, humility, and compassion.

The future of our country rests in our hands. For me, as a Christian, giving up hope is never an option. I dare to believe that God will never give up on us, and that with God's help, we can rise to the challenges before us.

I hope that you will find inspiration in the stories of how others learned to be brave and realize that all great heroes once stood on the same threshold of youth. Most importantly, I pray that you will be encouraged to trust your inner voice in the decisive moments that will set you on the path of your destiny.

Courage is contagious. Together, with God's help, we can learn to be brave. Together we can work for good in this world.

FOREWORD

It started with about ten people tagging me on social media.

"Do you know Bishop Budde?"

"Aren't you a priest?"

"What the heck is an Episcopalian?"

(Answers: "Kinda." "Yep." "That's complicated.")

Bishop Mariann Edgar Budde's homily "A Service of Prayer for the Nation" had struck a collective nerve, from dyed-in-the-wool Episcopalians to Catholics and atheists—all the way up to the Oval Office, it seemed. Despite the social-media fervor, I didn't have time to watch the sermon right away. It was the start of a new semester at my teaching job at a school just outside of Minneapolis, Minnesota, so things were busy. Still, I made a mental note to go back and listen to Bishop Budde's sermon, but, honestly, I've listened to—and preached—countless sermons in my life. Very few rise to the level of "Wow, that impacted me!" let alone tagging friends online or starting any sort of widespread public conversation.

Sermons—much like live theater—are almost always directed to and created for a very specific group of people in a very specific time and place. So I was surprised when, later that evening, the conversation was not only still happening but had picked up steam. People were *excited*. They were emboldened. And perhaps most importantly, they were validated in their fears and worries around the second term of newly sworn in president Donald Trump. As the intensity grew, I started to wonder what Bishop Budde had said in this sermon.

Had she invoked one of the more radical Christian voices? James Cone? Dietrich Bonhoeffer? Dorothy Day, perhaps? Had she, from the pulpit of the National Cathedral, called for a radical, jubilee moment? The sort prescribed in the Hebrew Scriptures, where the land is restored, slaves are freed, debts are forgiven, ailments are healed, and we know once and for all that God's ultimate restoration of creation is not merely a hope, but a *promise*—a promise that reminds us of God's grace and forgiveness as well as the importance of social justice and equity on this side of the Jordan . . .

But I have ADHD. So I spent my night playing video games, fiddling with my mountain bike, and stringing a fishing rod until, shockingly, I looked up and it was past midnight. I thought, "Okay, I will watch her sermon tomorrow."

The next morning, my inbox was full of even more questions about the Episcopal Church, and what it meant to be a bishop, and whether she would face any sort of repercussions from the broader church for her message. My imagination was running wild now. I had visions of an epic, adversarial sermon—one where the good bishop stood high in the pulpit and condemned President Trump and his administration.

How could anything less than that bring about this sort of commentary and attention?

The Episcopal Church hasn't often drawn a spotlight like this. Like many mainline Protestant traditions, we are suffering from a rapid decline in membership and from a general lack of interest in our Main Guy—Jesus. This, of course, has nothing to do with Jesus. Instead, it's the product of a church that has not listened to the culture—a church that has made mistakes, not the least of which is forgetting what I would argue is a cardinal rule for anyone who follows a particular faith tradition:

It has to matter.

Bishop Budde had struck a nerve. Suddenly, it mattered.

As I drove to school, I queued up the recording and waited with expectation for the bishop to get radical. Fifteen minutes later, sitting in the parking lot of my school, I was confused.

Had I listened to the wrong sermon?

It wasn't that the homily was *bad*—not at all. It was just . . . tame? Well, as tame as the radically subversive Gospel of Christ can be. But I had heard sermons like this my entire life, not only in the often liberal-leaning Episcopal Church, but also in the more conservative Southern Methodist churches of my youth and young adulthood.

Bishop Budde preached about mercy. ("Empathy" would later be a word added to the mix, though it doesn't actually appear in the sermon.) *Mercy.* She simply asked for mercy, and it had kicked off a maelstrom like I had not seen in the church maybe ever. As I sat in my truck, I tried to figure out why this had landed in such a dramatic way.

That morning, I followed the rapidly building discourse around the homily and the response from President Trump. He questioned Budde's consecration as bishop while delivering the usual personal attacks on her character, position, and gender. Still, I was at a loss. Colleagues asked my thoughts and I admitted that, while the sermon was good, I never would've expected this reaction. I spent the day befuddled.

Then a student showed up in my classroom. This particular student—a basketball player, confident and popular—came in uncharacteristically shyly and quietly asked me about the sermon. He paused, shuffled his feet, and looked back out the door.

"Is that what we are about?"

My school is rooted in Episcopal identity, which makes us not dissimilar to Catholic or other Christian schools, except that we do not base our identity on *belief* as much as *values.* Essentially, this means that you and I can sit in the same pew and have drastically different ideas about God and the world, but because we are part of a community, we are bound to one another in ways that defy and often conflict with how the world thinks about restoration, reconciliation, and what it means to be powerful.

The *how* of our belief, or the ways we are called to act in the world, comes from the Baptismal Covenant. Found in the *Book of Common Prayer*, the Baptismal Covenant is both an individual promise and a community agreement that says to the person being baptized—often a baby who cannot understand the gravity of such promises—that we will be there with you *no matter what*.

This is a big statement, one that is perhaps bigger than we want to actually believe. Because if you believe it, suddenly you cannot stand by when other people are being harmed or marginalized. You cannot deny the *dignity* of all people. Read that again: *all people*, no matter their race, creed, orientation, pronouns, whether they are a lowly Green Bay Packers fan—*nothing*.

This was the importance of Bishop Budde's sermon. It was a clear reminder that God always sides with the oppressed, the marginalized—the widow and the refugee. It's a topic that, despite what politicians might tell you, is *fundamental* to the Christian belief system. I would go so far as to say you cannot be Christian and deny help to the least of these.

In the weeks that followed, the discourse turned what can only be described as *bananas*. Suddenly, conservative talking heads were telling us about the *sin of empathy* and about why empathy and mercy, in fact, were not part of the Christian message but, instead, were nothing more than a thinly veiled Marxist plot to corrupt the church—and the entire country.

I hope you see the ridiculousness, and maybe the fear, in such arguments.

Christians are undeniably called to mercy, empathy, and compassion. Christians are called to resist the ideals and expectations of Empire, namely, that we only are only responsible for ourselves in a world where vengeance is confused with justice.

This resistance, I think, is the real power of Bishop Budde's message. It was a compassionate and clear reminder of this different way, one that refused to bow down even in the face of the highest office of our country.

At this specific time and place, her sermon makes me proud to be an Episcopalian, let alone a priest. And in my capacity as both chaplain and teacher at my school, it's a burning reminder of the stakes involved when we invoke the big questions of ethics and theology, when we ask teenagers and young people to care about Ultimate Things.

Or maybe the best way to describe it is in the answer I gave to the basketball player who came into my office. The answer I gave him is the answer I will give you as you begin to read about Bishop Budde and the important process of learning how to be brave:

"This is what we are about."

Reverend Bryan Bliss

Easter, 2025

MARIANN EDGAR BUDDE

ON JANUARY 21, 2025
WASHINGTON NATIONAL CATHEDRAL

Jesus said, "Everyone then who hears these words of mine and acts on them will be like a wise man who built his house on rock. The rain fell, the floods came, and the winds blew and beat on that house, but it did not fall, because it had been founded on rock. And everyone who hears these words of mine and does not act on them will be like a foolish man who built his house on sand. The rain fell, and the floods came, and the winds blew and beat against that house, and it fell—and great was its fall!" Now when Jesus had finished saying these things, the crowds were astounded at his teaching, for he taught them as one having authority, and not as their scribes.

Matthew 7:24–29

Joined by many across the country, we have gathered this morning to pray for unity as a nation—not for agreement, political or otherwise, but for the kind of unity that fosters community across diversity and division, a unity that serves the common good.

Unity, in this sense, is the threshold requirement for people to live together in a free society, it is the solid rock, as Jesus said, in this case upon which to build a nation. It is not conformity. It is not a victory of one over another. It is not weary politeness nor passivity born of exhaustion. Unity is not partisan.

Rather, unity is a way of being with one another that encompasses and respects differences, that teaches us to hold multiple perspectives and life experiences as valid and worthy of respect; that enables us, in our communities and in the halls of power, to genuinely care for one another even when we disagree. Those across our country who dedicate their lives, or who volunteer, to help others in times of natural disaster, often at great risk to themselves, never ask those they are helping for whom they voted in the past election or what positions they hold on a particular issue. We are at our best when we follow their example.

Unity at times is sacrificial, in the way that love is sacrificial, a giving of ourselves for the sake of another. Jesus of Nazareth, in his Sermon on the Mount, exhorts us to love not only our neighbors, but to love our enemies, and to pray for those who persecute us; to be merciful, as our God is merciful, and to forgive others, as God forgives us. Jesus went out of his way to welcome those whom his society deemed as outcasts.

Now, I grant you that unity, in this broad, expansive sense, is aspirational, and it's a lot to pray for—a big ask of our God, worthy of the best of who we are and can be. But there isn't much to be gained by our prayers if we act in ways that further deepen and exploit the divisions among us. Our Scriptures are quite clear that God is never impressed with prayers when actions are not informed by them. Nor does God spare us from the consequences of our deeds, which, in the end, matter more than the words we pray.

Those of us gathered here in this cathedral are not naive about the realities of politics. When power, wealth, and competing interests are at stake; when views of what America should be are in conflict; when there are strong opinions across a spectrum of possibilities and starkly different understandings of what the right course of action is, there will be winners and losers when votes are cast or decisions made that set the course of public policy and the prioritization of resources. It goes without saying that in a democracy, not everyone's particular hopes and dreams will be realized in a given legislative session or a presidential term or even a generation. Not everyone's specific prayers—for those of us who are people of prayer—will be answered as we would like. But for some, the loss of their hopes and dreams will be far more than political defeat, but instead a loss of equality, dignity, and livelihood.

Given this, is true unity among us even possible? And why should we care about it?

Well, I hope that we care, because the culture of contempt that has become normalized in our country threatens to destroy us.[1] We

---

1   I am indebted to Tim Shriver, CEO & Founder of Project Unite, for introducing me to the concept of a "culture of contempt" and how a focus on human dignity is a positive alternative that allows us to speak respectfully to one another across difference.

are all bombarded daily with messages from what sociologists now call "the outrage industrial complex,"[2] some of it driven by external forces whose interests are furthered by a polarized America. Contempt fuels our political campaigns and social media, and many profit from it. But it's a dangerous way to lead a country.

I am a person of faith, and with God's help I believe that unity in this country is possible—not perfectly, for we are imperfect people and an imperfect union—but sufficient enough to keep us believing in and working to realize the ideals of the United States of America—ideals expressed in the Declaration of Independence, with its assertion of innate human equality and dignity.

And we are right to pray for God's help as we seek unity, for we need God's help, but only if we ourselves are willing to tend to the foundations upon which unity depends. Like Jesus' analogy of building a house of faith on the rock of his teachings, as opposed to building a house on sand, the foundations we need for unity must be sturdy enough to withstand the many storms that threaten it.

What are the foundations of unity? Drawing from our sacred traditions and texts, let me suggest that there are at least three.

The first foundation for unity is honoring the inherent dignity of every human being, which is, as all faiths represented here affirm, the birthright of all people as children of the One God. In public discourse, honoring each other's dignity means refusing to

---

2   https://law.stanford.edu/2019/12/20/the-outrage-industrial-complex/

mock, discount, or demonize those with whom we differ, choosing instead to respectfully debate across our differences, and whenever possible, to seek common ground. If common ground is not possible, dignity demands that we remain true to our convictions without contempt for those who hold convictions of their own.

A second foundation for unity is honesty in both private conversation and public discourse. If we aren't willing to be honest, there is no use in praying for unity, because our actions work against the prayers themselves. We might, for a time, experience a false sense of unity among some, but not the sturdier, broader unity that we need to address the challenges we face.

Now, to be fair, we don't always know where the truth lies, and there is a lot working against the truth now, staggeringly so. But when we do know what is true, it's incumbent upon us to speak the truth, even when—and especially when—it costs us.

A third foundation for unity is humility, which we all need, because we are all fallible human beings. We make mistakes. We say and do things that we regret. We have our blind spots and biases, and we are perhaps the most dangerous to ourselves and others when we are persuaded, without a doubt, that we are *absolutely right* and someone else is *absolutely wrong*. Because then we are just a few steps away from labeling ourselves as the good people, versus the bad people.

The truth is that we are all people, capable of both good and bad. Aleksandr Solzhenitsyn astutely observed that "The line separating good and evil passes not through states, nor between classes, nor between political parties—but right through every human heart—and through all human hearts."[3]

The more we realize this, the more room we have within ourselves for humility, and openness to one another across our differences, because in fact, we are more like one another than we realize, and we need each other.

Unity is relatively easy to pray for on occasions of solemnity. It's a lot harder to realize when we're dealing with real differences in the public arena. But without unity, we are building our nation's house on sand.

With a commitment to unity that incorporates diversity and transcends disagreement, and the solid foundations of dignity, honesty, and humility that such unity requires, we can do our part, in our time, to help realize the ideals and the dream of America.

Let me make one final plea, Mr. President. Millions have put their trust in you. As you told the nation yesterday, you have felt the providential hand of a loving God. In the name of our God, I ask you to have mercy upon the people in our country who are scared now. There are gay, lesbian, and transgender children in Republican, Democratic, and independent families, some of whom fear for their lives.

And the people who pick our crops and clean our office buildings; who labor in our poultry farms and meat-packing plants; who

---

3   Aleksandr Solzhenitsyn, *The Gulag Archipelago, 1918–1956*

wash the dishes after we eat in restaurants and work the night shift in hospitals—they may not be citizens or have the proper documentation, but the vast majority of immigrants are not criminals. They pay taxes, and are good neighbors. They are faithful members of our churches, mosques and synagogues, gurdwaras, and temples.

Have mercy, Mr. President, on those in our communities whose children fear that their parents will be taken away. Help those who are fleeing war zones and persecution in their own lands to find compassion and welcome here. Our God teaches us that we are to be merciful to the stranger, for we were once strangers in this land.

May God grant us all the strength and courage to honor the dignity of every human being, speak the truth in love, and walk humbly with one another and our God, for the good of all the people of this nation and the world.

CHAPTER ONE

DECIDING TO GO

Now the Lord said to Abram, "Go from your country and your kindred and your father's house to the land that I will show you." —*Genesis 12:1*

We learn who we are by telling stories. There is none more familiar or beloved than the **hero's journey**, the tale of one who bravely decides to go into the unknown.

It is a universal narrative, spanning time and culture. Yet as the spiritual writer Henri Nouwen once observed, "the most personal is the most universal, the most hidden is the most public, and the most solitary is the most communal."

LEARN ABOUT IT

The hero's journey is a storytelling formula that describes a "hero's" adventure, trials, and ultimate transformation. It was popularized by Joseph Campbell in his 1949 book, *The Hero with a Thousand Faces*, where he outlines a structure that is seen in countless books, movies, and other stories. The hero leaves home, faces obstacles, receives assistance, achieves a goal, and by the end of the story has returned home transformed.

Hearing another person's **courageous journey**, we can't help but consider our own.

The call to go is often a definitive moment in our lives. But it's understandable if we hesitate. The decision to go involves leaving one place and going to another. It can mean releasing familiar relationships for the unknown, all in service of an enormous task. It is risky, and the cost is high. Yet we go because we are convinced that such sacrifice is necessary to fulfill a destiny that lies beyond our sight.

The journey often begins long before we take the first step. The call to go beyond what is comfortable often catches us by surprise, and there is almost always resistance—from ourselves or from people who want us to stay where we are.

Being completely ready is rare.

Like baby birds that need to be pushed out of the nest, we often don't know we have wings until we're forced to fly.

LEARN ABOUT IT

Henri Nouwen (1932–1996) was a priest, theologian, and writer known for his spiritual writings on topics like solitude, compassion, and vulnerability. He is best known for his work with those living on the margins of society, particularly during his time at L'Arche Daybreak, a community for people with intellectual disabilities.

WHEN I WAS A JUNIOR in high school, my family life fell apart. By then I had learned to keep my emotions in separate boxes as a way to keep the overwhelming sense of fear at a distance. I was used to constant anxiety about money, lack of affection, and periodic blowups, followed by stretches of uneasy quiet that allowed me to focus on other things.

When my father told me he was leaving my stepmother—and said I could come with him—I'm pretty sure he expected me to say yes. He didn't mention my eight-year-old half brother, Jim. I wasn't surprised. In the mostly silent war between our parents, our father saw me as his ally, while my stepmother fiercely claimed her son. Assuming I was on his side, my father asked me to keep his plan between us. I reluctantly agreed, not knowing that he had already called a moving company. My stepmother learned about his decision a few days later when she came home to a half-empty house.

There was no way I was going anywhere with my father alone. I didn't know then what clinical depression or alcoholism was, but I saw their effects in him. His sense of intimacy with me was pure fantasy and more than a little frightening. Staying with my stepmother wasn't an option either, although I think that she, too, imagined I would. When I told her I wasn't going to stay with her, she insisted that I move out immediately. I wanted freedom more than anything, even if it meant the difficult decision to leave my brother behind.

I knew I had to go, and I knew where.

My mother lived in New Jersey, where my sister, Christine, and I were raised before our parents' painful and messy divorce. In the custody battle, I played a significant role in both the pain and the mess. When our father made a move to gain custody of Christine, I didn't want to be left behind. In the family judge's chambers, I exaggerated stories of our life in New Jersey, thinking it would please our father. He was indeed pleased when the judge awarded him custody of us both, citing what I said as a determining factor in his decision. Our mother was shattered.

Looking back, I'm stunned by my capacity for cruelty. Why did I say those things to hurt our mother? I knew that she loved us. What I remember was the panic I felt thinking about Christine moving to Colorado without me. I was weary of looking into the windows of other families, wondering what it would be like to belong to them. Our mother was gone a lot, working full-time while going to school. Only later did I realize how focused she was on our survival and how alone she was in her grief. In an era when all my friends seemed to have intact families, I hated the word *divorced*. Our dad, stepmother, and new baby brother seemed to offer the normality I craved.

It was an illusion. Our time in Colorado was rocky from the start. Within months, Christine's life spun out of control, and after two tumultuous years, she left home for good. Our father tried his hand at several business ventures and failed at them all, eventually declaring bankruptcy and consoling himself with alcohol as our stepmother frantically tried to make ends meet and protect her son.

By the end of my sophomore year, I had disengaged from the drama and created an alternative family with a small circle of friends. They were Christians, and to my quiet amazement, so was I. Together we attended Young Life, a gathering of Christian teenagers that met weekly at our music teacher's house. At that teacher's invitation, we joined a touring choir, and some of us began attending the church that sponsored it. Outside of family, life continued to get better. The boy I had not-so-secretly adored finally noticed me. I discovered another home in the high school music department, and in the fall of my junior year, I was cast as a main character in our school's musical.

I knew, at last, what it felt like to belong.

So, when my family in Colorado collapsed, it broke my heart to think about leaving. My life was full of joy and meaning. While I was grateful that I had a mother to return to, it also felt as if I were standing at the edge of a cliff.

The choice was mine to make, but it also felt as if the decision was being made for me. The decision-maker, however, wasn't any of the authority figures in my life. Most of them wanted to help me finish high school in Colorado, including my church's pastor and his wife, who invited me to live with them. For the first time I can remember, I heard what I have come to identify as the voice of God speaking directly to my heart, even though my heart desperately wanted a different word.

I ultimately left on my own terms, which meant staying in Colorado long enough to perform in the musical and say goodbye to my friends, some of whom had begun their first year of college. I accepted the pastor's invitation and moved in with his family for two months and completed the fall semester.

When I said goodbye to my stepmother and brother, Jim wouldn't look at me or let me hug him. My father invited me to dinner in his basement apartment, and we ate his specialty at the time—macaroni with Velveeta Cheese and hot dogs. When it came time to go, my friends drove me to the airport, escorted me to the gate and onto the tarmac (you used to be able to do this!) gave me a bouquet of flowers, and waved as I climbed the stairs.

I cried all the way to New Jersey.

At that time, I didn't know Eleanor Roosevelt's definition of courage: doing what you think you cannot do. But that's what I did. Still, I had no illusion that returning to live with my mother would be easy. Returning would require some sort of reckoning, even if she had become an increasingly steady source of support while we were apart. She telephoned every Sunday evening I was in Colorado. For years, our conversations were brief and awkward, yet she persisted in love. She was growing surer of herself, more relaxed and grounded in her profession and in her faith. She found inspiration and community in the Episcopal Church. I don't remember how I asked if I could return to her, only that when the subject came up, she said yes.

In the end, what most prepared me for this decisive moment was the growing tension I felt about the Christian faith. My pastor back in Colorado fretted that I would **"backslide"** if I returned to the Episcopal Church of my childhood. I had no such worries. In fact, I was relieved to be released from a version of Christianity that I had secretly questioned more each day.

The truth is, I never doubted the

> # LEARN
> ## ABOUT IT
>
> In Christianity, the idea of "backsliding" represents moving away from God and toward a more "sinful" or worldly lifestyle. However, not all Christians believe in this idea. Traditions such as the Episcopal Church focus on grace, restoration, and the ongoing journey of faith rather than failure.

reality of God or the presence of Jesus in my life. I didn't question the sincerity of the people in my church. They were kind, loving, and dedicated to their Lord. It was the rigidity of their belief system that I struggled with, and their certainty that God's unconditional love was extended only to those who accepted Jesus as their personal savior in the precise way they did. There was no room for different experiences or understanding, or language to talk about the reality of human sin and brokenness that persisted after being saved. There certainly wasn't room for doubt.

I'm not sure I would have resolved that tension had I stayed in Colorado. Leaving the church that had nurtured me felt like an act of rebellion, but I knew I was being faithful to God in a way that I hadn't experienced before. The conflict wasn't lost on me. I felt no need to judge or criticize my church, and yet I knew I didn't fit in their world. I was grateful for what they had given me, but I silently rejected most of what they taught. It was the first time it dawned on me that a relationship with God isn't defined by "correct" beliefs but rather a willingness to trust and step out in faith. **Without realizing it, I left Colorado in search of a more expansive understanding of God.** As grace would have it, I found what I didn't know I was looking for in the Episcopal Church of my childhood.

Not everything resulting from that decision was positive. In going, I abandoned my younger brother, and our relationship never fully recovered. I have learned that every decision, even the most life-affirming, carries the weight of consequences. All I knew then was that there were reasons beyond my understanding for me to go, and that my life depended on taking the first steps toward a future I could not see.

Life transitions, however, are usually not neat and predictable. They can come at any time, often when we least expect them, and

---

THINK
ABOUT IT

Beliefs are a set of principles, rules, or ideas you live your life by and often influence how we treat other people. They can be religious or not, but everyone has beliefs, whether it's "*Die Hard* is *not* a Christmas movie" or "God loves the world." Our beliefs come from religion, family, and experience. But what happens if a strongly held belief is challenged? Should beliefs be adaptable?

we learn to take them in stride. Author Bruce Feiler describes this moment as a "lifequake," a transition of such magnitude that it fundamentally changes our meaning, purpose, or direction. Over a lifetime, we may undergo dozens of transitions, but only a few rise to the level of a lifequake. During a lifequake, we know something big is happening, but it still takes time to grasp and accept that there is no going back.

More than four thousand years ago, Abraham—a spiritual ancestor claimed by Judaism, Christianity, and Islam—heard a voice inside telling him to leave his home and settle in a new land. If he did, he would become the father of a nation.

The **biblical narrative** begins in the book of Genesis with stories of how God created the universe and of humankind's fall from grace. Adam and Eve, Noah's ark, Cain and Abel, the Tower of Babel—they all have a universal perspective, for all peoples of the earth. Then in Genesis, chapter 12, the focus abruptly shifts to one couple, Abraham and Sarah. Their journey marks the birth of a new people called and set apart by God.

Abraham was very old, and his

LEARN
ABOUT IT

Biblical stories can be described as archetypes of "myths." But this does not mean they are untrue. In fact, a myth often *loses* its true meaning if taken literally. Instead, think of myths as a different way of seeing—they are true not in the way that formulas are true, but instead how a work of art is True. They don't explain *how* something occurred but instead help us think about *why* life is the way it is at a given time.

wife, Sarah, could not have children. God's call to them was specific: fashion an alternative community in a world gone awry.

The decisive moment to *go* could not be more immediate:

> *Now the Lord said to Abram, "Go from your country and your kindred and your father's house to the land that I will show you. I will make of you a great nation, and I will bless you, and make your name great, so that you will be a blessing. I will bless those who bless you, . . . and in you all the families of the earth shall be blessed."* **So Abram went, as the Lord had told him** *[emphasis added]*.

There is no inner turmoil or doubt, no wrestling with angels or demons, no arguing with God. The childless and elderly Abram, who is later given the name Abraham, has a vision that involves bearing children, a promise so outlandish that Sarah laughs when she hears it for herself. Still, she joins him.

They go.

Given the matter-of-fact description of Abraham and Sarah's decision to go, it's easy to miss its significance. Abraham simply does what the Lord commands. Their journey has twists and turns born of human frailty and political conflict. Both Abraham and Sarah make dreadful decisions and cause harm to those closest to them. Yet their mistakes and moral failings do not negate God's promise or diminish the significance of that first decisive moment when they said *yes*.

Like Abraham and Sarah, we never feel more alive than when we take a leap of faith. Their story can be a template for us, to help us trust those rare experiences of clarity when they come. The fact that the text doesn't tell us what Abraham and Sarah felt is a helpful reminder that in our decisive moments, our feelings—or anyone else's—are surprisingly irrelevant.

What matters is whether we choose to hear and accept the call.

JOSEPH CAMPBELL ASSURES US the hero's journey is not meant for the few.

"Heroes have a thousand faces," he writes, and one of them is ours. Yet reasons to stay are everywhere. Leaving is hard. When we go, a part of us dies and we must give up a *past* version of ourselves to *become* the person waiting for us on the other side. In classic coming-of-age stories, the first step is often in response to situations beyond the hero's control. Think of Dorothy in *The Wizard of Oz* blown out of Kansas by a tornado. At first, most young heroes resist the call and only reluctantly consent later. In *The Lord of the Rings*, Frodo wishes that the evil One Ring had never come to him. Sometimes the journey begins with liberation, as it does for Harry Potter, freed from the miseries of 4 Privet Drive when he steps onto the train bound for Hogwarts.

Along the way, our heroes meet significant mentors, cross important thresholds, experience great trials, and have at least one transformative crisis. Sometimes they go on to new lands, while at other times they return home with wisdom to impart. The hero's journey is both intensely personal, the foundation of a life distinctly and meaningfully lived, and of communal importance, for the call is never for self alone. The effects of a courageous, faithful life reverberate across time and space.

The first decisions to go, especially in young adulthood, stand out in our memory as critical moments in the development of our identities. Eventually, these become who we are and create patterns that, when the heroic journey calls us again, we lean on for their familiarity.

LEARN
ABOUT IT

Howard Thurman (1899–1981) was a theologian, author, and civil rights leader whose writings and social-justice-focused Christianity engaged a variety of spiritual traditions, including the work and ideas of Mahatma Gandhi, as he looked for ways to connect faith with social

IN 1943, an important sense of purpose came for Black American pastor and educator **Howard Thurman** when he was invited to go to San Francisco to co-lead a newly forming interracial Christian community.

Thurman had been among the first Black Americans to cross the color line in the Jim Crow era. He was a sought-after preacher in both Black and white churches and a frequent speaker at religious conferences, although often denied service at the hotels where they took place. Over the years, he grew increasingly impatient with American Christianity's unwillingness to confront racism within its churches and justice. His work was the spark for countless theologians and activists, including the Reverend Dr. Martin Luther King Jr. society at large. He drew a distinction between what he called the "genius of the religion of Jesus" and the practice of Christianity as he had experienced it in the United States.

Born in 1899, Thurman had long recognized a call to help dismantle racism in the church, even in seemingly impossible circumstances. He grew up in the segregated city of Daytona, Florida. His father died when he was seven, and as all Black children were then and are today, he was forced to navigate the evils of racism at an early age. Yet he was blessed to be raised by loving adults and nurtured in a protective church community. His elementary school teachers recognized his intelligence and helped him continue his education beyond seventh grade, when public school for Black American children ended. These positive influences instilled in him, as he would later write, a strong sense that his life and what he did with it mattered.

In childhood and adolescence, Thurman found solace and strength in nature, inspiration from his family and teachers, and a fierce desire to study—forces that enabled him to overcome innumerable obstacles. At every step, his singular focus, obvious brilliance, and personal sacrifice, aided by the sacrifices others

**LEARN
ABOUT IT**

In Christianity, grace is
the overwhelming and
unmerited love of God. It
is a reminder that there
is nothing for us to do but
accept God's love and
then offer it to others.

willingly made on his behalf, gave him a sense of purpose and responsibility.

Thurman experienced **grace**—mystical encounters mediated through the natural world or the kindness of strangers—that persuaded him that God had something to do with the doors that had opened for him at opportune moments.

A hint that he would be called to go to San Francisco occurred ten years earlier while he was on pilgrimage in India. Thurman and his wife, Sue Bailey Thurman, were leading a delegation of Black Americans on a mission of friendship organized by the World Student Christian Federation. Mahatma Gandhi's nonviolent movement against British colonial rule had captured the world's attention. The Thurmans' three-hour conversation with Gandhi confirmed Howard's conviction that nonviolence was the only way to overcome racial injustice in the United States. "It may be through the Negroes," Gandhi said to Thurman as his parting blessing and exhortation, "that the unadulterated message of nonviolence will be delivered to the world."

While on a sightseeing visit to the Khyber Pass, part of the ancient trade route through a rugged mountain range between modern-day Afghanistan and Pakistan that enabled the exchange of ideas, culture, and faiths from many lands, Thurman was given a vision: "to create a religious fellowship that was capable of cutting across all racial barriers." For years afterward, he held close the prospect of establishing a truly interracial expression of Christianity that would celebrate the wondrous diversity of humankind.

Thurman's decision to leave an esteemed position at Howard University, the flagship academic institution for Black Americans, to start an interracial church puzzled those around him. Howard's dean pressed him to consider the risks he was taking, not only for himself but also for his family. Thurman wrote to his counterpart in San Francisco, "There are risks involved in our bold venture and we must be prepared to take our share of them." This was his chance to create a church that was worthy of Jesus. There was nothing easy in the work to establish what became the Fellowship Church. Yet Thurman never expected it to be easy, and for another ten years he poured everything he had into the church. It was a time of fulfillment and frustration. It was a time of satisfaction and disappointment. The Fellowship's ministry in San Francisco was influential, but it didn't have the national impact he had hoped.

It was during this time of intense focus on pastoring a relatively small congregation when he published his most influential book, *Jesus and the Disinherited*.

LEARN
ABOUT IT

Jesus and the Disinherited examines the Christian Gospels through the lens of oppressed and marginalized peoples—or "the disinherited." Thurman believed that because Jesus was a member of an oppressed group, he understood and spoke directly to the experience of suffering. As a result, liberation from the forces of oppression, through the power of love and self-worth, are key tools for the work of fighting oppression.

Thurman would hear the call to go once more, in 1953, to assume a leadership position at Boston University, a historically white institution. He was reluctant to leave Fellowship Church, which he considered the most significant accomplishment of his life. Yet he also felt a responsibility to rising generations and was persuaded that a university would offer the widest possible platform for his message of nonviolent resistance. It was at Boston University where a young doctoral student named Martin Luther King Jr. first encountered Thurman, who would remain his spiritual inspiration for life.

YEARS AGO, a good friend heard the call to change professions in midlife. Her new vocation would require significant education, with a corresponding loss of income. It would also involve moving, with or without her family, to another city for a year of on-site learning. The resistance to this call, both within and around her, was intense. Even after she made the decision, she wavered for more than a year. It was an agonizing time, as she held both the call and all that worked against it.

Then one day, something shifted inside her, and she was clear in a way that she hadn't felt before. She continued to be gracious and considerate of her family, but she no longer doubted that it was time to go. When I asked her about the change, she simply said, "I knew that it was time. It's not going to be easy, but not going simply wasn't an option."

The decisive moment had come.

Such clarity, when and however it comes, is a gift—whether it's the first or the hundredth time we feel it. Whether we go in fear or excitement, we feel as if our lives matter. In fear, we are given the courage to do what we think we cannot do. In excitement, it's as if we had been preparing our whole lives for this moment.

And if the cost of going is high? Well, it merely confirms the importance of the call.

This feeling first came to me at age seventeen, and I can count on one hand the times I have felt it since. But that initial experience—aided by examples of courage found in scripture, history, and literature, and in the lives of those I've met—reminds me that when the heroic journey presents itself, I will recognize it and know what to do.

I believe that you will too.

CHAPTER TWO

DECIDING TO STAY

Here I stand, I can do no other, so help me God. —Martin Luther

Ian Bedloe is the seventeen-year-old protagonist of Anne Tyler's 1991 novel, *Saint Maybe*. He blames himself for the death of his older brother, Danny, and the family tragedies that follow. One evening, as he wanders the streets of his home city of Baltimore, Ian sees a neon sign in a storefront window: "Church of the Second Chance." He takes his place among a small group of people, and hears himself telling them about his brother's death—and his guilt.

The minister, the Reverend Emmett, a kind yet spiritually rigid young man, assures Ian that forgiveness is possible, provided that he **atones** for his sins. So, Ian decides to drop out of school and take a menial job to help provide

LEARN ABOUT IT

The idea of atonement is rooted in reconciliation. In Christianity, this occurs in the work of Jesus Christ on the cross.

In Judaism, Yom Kippur (the Day of Atonement) is a day of reflection, repentance, and seeking forgiveness. While atonement theories can vary across different religions—and inside the same religion!—it is fundamentally a way of theologically understanding and seeking forgiveness, making amends, and restoring broken relationships.

for his brother's children. Years go by as he works each day, cares for his family, and is a faithful member of the church. Still, the forgiveness that he longs for eludes him, and he begins to question the choices he has made.

Sensing that Ian is troubled, the Reverend Emmett offers to walk him home from church one Sunday afternoon. As they walk, all of Ian's frustrations pour out of him. "I'm wasting my life," he declares. The Reverend Emmett stops and turns to look directly into Ian's eyes. "This *is* your life," he says. "Lean into it . . . View your burden as a gift. It's the theme that has been given you to work with . . . This is the only life you'll have."

Given the drama, adrenaline, and outward energy involved in deciding to go, *staying* can feel like being trapped. Yet the decision to stay also can be brave and consequential. In fact, there is often a similar internal struggle and building sense of crisis, leading to a decisive moment, in both going and staying. But there the similarity ends. Deciding to stay means choosing to go deeper into the life we already have.

The call to go is often associated with the adventurous side of courage. So, choosing to stay can appear as if we are settling for less. Yet staying often creates depth, which often leads to creating lasting differences in the lives of others. In choosing to stay, we acknowledge that there is more at stake than what we feel or want. We learn that there is more than one way to live a brave life and that some of the most courageous decisions we make are ones that no one sees.

When I first read *Saint Maybe*, the Reverend Emmett's words to Ian felt like God's words to me: "This is your life. Stay where you are."

Until then, my life had been largely defined by going—moving from one place to the next, stepping out of one world and into another, learning to be brave in the face of the unknown. I've had to learn, time and again, that faithfulness isn't always about taking big leaps, but is also walking with small steps, and that it's possible to make a lasting difference in the world by tending to one small corner of it.

One summer, I traveled with my husband and our young child, Amos, to Sweden, joining my mother on her annual trek home. We stayed at the rustic farm that her parents bought after World War II and where my Swedish family gathers in the warmer months. It's a beautiful spot, and we were welcomed warmly. Yet within a week, I felt restless. I wanted to travel the country, hike, and tour other parts of Europe. Instead, every day Amos and I walked down a dirt path to watch the neighbor's sheep graze. He would stand there for what felt like hours, and

I stood next to him, trying to fight off the envy I felt for those who could simply *go*.

That same summer I stumbled upon *The Little Prince* by Antoine de Saint-Exupéry. It's a whimsical story filled with wisdom about the quirks of human nature. The Little Prince rules on a small planet known as Asteroid 325. On that planet there also lives a single rose, which the Little Prince loves even though her pretentiousness and need for constant affection causes him grief. To cure his wounded heart, the Little Prince decides to leave his rose and travel the galaxy.

After he lands on Earth, the Little Prince climbs a mountain so that he might get a better view. From the top he sees hundreds of roses in a garden, a revelation that causes him to sit down and weep. His rose had assured him that she was special and that it was a privilege to love her. But here in one garden alone there are hundreds just like her.

If she is but an ordinary rose, who, then, is he?

The Little Prince meets a fox who teaches him an invaluable lesson.

"To me," the fox says, "you are nothing more than a little boy who is just like a hundred thousand other little boys. I have no need of you. And you have no need of me. I am just a fox, like a hundred thousand other foxes. But if you tame me, then we shall need each other. To me, you will be unique in all the world, and I will be the same for you."

The Little Prince realizes that the same is true about the roses in the garden. For all their beauty, he does not love them. He loves the single rose on his tiny planet that he watered, sheltered, and cared for. "It is the time you have spent with your rose that makes her so important," the fox tells the Little Prince. "You are responsible for your rose."

"You are responsible for your rose" has become a personal mantra. It reminds me of the sacredness of all the people, such as my son Amos, who are entrusted to my care. Presbyterian minister **Frederick Buechner** also taught me a similar lesson on the value of stability.

Buechner writes this:

LEARN ABOUT IT

Frederick Buechner (1926–2022) was an American writer, Presbyterian minister, and theologian whose books—which included novels, memoirs, and traditional theology—help readers look for the sacred in everyday life.

> *If I were called upon to state in a few words the essence of everything I was trying to say both as a novelist and a preacher it would be something like this: Listen to your life. See it for the fathomless mystery that it is. In the boredom and pain of it no less than in the excitement and gladness: touch, taste, and smell your way to the holy and hidden heart of it because in the last analysis all moments are key moments, and life itself is grace.*

That summer I began listening as hard as I could, learning

day by day what it meant to be, as the author of the psalms in the Christian and Hebrew Bibles writes, "like trees planted by streams of water, which yield their fruit in its season, and their leaves do not wither." It has become a lifelong practice, one that requires constant renewal. Because the days spent *staying* far outnumber those *going*. It's a reminder that there is nothing inherently complacent or fearful in choosing to stay. Of course, I do not mean to suggest that staying in abusive or harmful situations is God's will, or that self-sacrifice is always the path of love. However, in the right situation, the faithfulness of staying can be nothing short of heroic.

Benedictine nun Joan Chittister, who brought contemporary language to **Saint Benedict's Rule**, reminds us of the importance of staying. Benedict established a monastic community in the tumultuous years of the sixth century, when the world seemed to be falling apart. He was grounded in the simple practices of daily life and the grace to be found in a healthy balance between work, prayer, study, and rest.

Reading *The Rule of Benedict* over the years has given me wisdom and grace to reorient my focus on where I am rather than where I think I want to

LEARN
ABOUT IT

The Rule of Benedict is a set of guidelines for monastic living, which emphasizes a life of prayer, work, and study— usually within a communal setting. The Rule emphasizes moderation and a focus on prayer and work that has provided a framework for Christian spirituality.

go. One sentence leapt out when I first read it and remains with me still:

> *"It may be the neighborhood we live in rather than the neighborhood we want that will really make human beings out of us."*

I sometimes hear in prayer or meditation an invitation to substitute the word **neighborhood** with whatever it is I'm struggling with, and its truth resounds. Where I am may, in fact, be where I need to be. What I want, although perhaps good and admirable, may not be possible or worth the cost.

THINK
ABOUT IT

What word do *you* substitute for *neighborhood* in the Benedictine prayer?

Pursuing our heart's desires can be the most life-affirming choice we can make, even when it takes us from other commitments. However, sometimes, we are asked to develop deep relationships and discover the sometimes-hidden treasures of longevity. There is a different kind of joy in being the one people can count on.

For all the goodness of staying, however, there are times when it isn't something we choose but rather must simply accept. When a door of opportunity closes, staying often feels like failure. Disappointment is unavoidable. But after a necessary time of grief, we realize that staying is often when seeds of new possibilities are planted and slowly take root. If we're not going anywhere, there is time and opportunity to tend to ourselves and hone our skills—to savor grace in small packages, and to learn perseverance.

At best, the decision to stay is a daily choice to remain whole-heartedly in one's life and commitments, resisting the temptation to simply drift through life. At the crossroads of staying or going, it takes courage to choose to understand what staying demands or makes possible.

A story in the Gospel of John speaks powerfully to these moments. It tells of a time when Jesus's teaching has become increasingly controversial, and the crowds that once hung on his every word begin to fall away. Even some of those closest to him no longer want to be part of his movement. "This teaching is difficult," they say. "Who can accept it?" In a moment of serious questioning, Jesus turns to the twelve disciples of his innermost circle and asks, "Do you also wish to go away?" His question hangs in the air. At last **Simon Peter** speaks up: "Lord, to whom would we go? You have the words of eternal life." They have come too far to turn back now. Their lives are bound up in his.

Time and again I have found my

LEARN ABOUT IT

Peter (originally named Simon) was a fisherman and one of Jesus Christ's twelve apostles. He is a major figure in the New Testament, known for his impulsive nature, deep faith, and moments of doubt. Peter was a major leader of the early church and played a significant role in spreading Christianity.

answer in Simon Peter's question: To whom would I go? I've come too far with Jesus to walk away. Although I am often discouraged by my own failings and those of others, I've never lost faith in Jesus, and I am forever inspired by those who live their lives by his light, and strive to be more like them.

And so I stay.

Another example—inspiration—is the Reverend Dr. Kelly Brown Douglas, the inaugural dean of the Episcopal Divinity School at Union Theological Seminary and canon theologian at Washington National Cathedral, author, and **womanist theologian**, a disciplined approach to theology that prioritizes the experience and perspectives of Black women. Douglas's writings show us that not all spiritual journeys follow a straight line. In the end, she decides to stay in the church despite the church's history of white supremacy and the harm it has inflicted.

LEARN
ABOUT IT

Womanist theology is a theological approach that centers the experience and work of Black women. It offers a lens through which to analyze and critique culture, including the church, in a context of gender, sexuality, and socioeconomic class. The novel *The Color Purple* by Alice Walker is a prime example of womanist theology.

As a child, Douglas attended the only Black Episcopal church in Dayton, Ohio. She loved church, and she especially loved hearing stories about Jesus. As she ventured beyond her congregation in adolescence, she was surprised to learn that not only were there white Episcopalians but that the church was predominantly white. Growing up, Douglas listened to her parents talk in hushed tones about racial violence. She once asked her father what Black people had done to make white people hate them.

By the time she reached college, she realized that the problem of white hatred didn't lie with Black people but within those determined to hate. She resolved to find some way to dedicate her life to dismantling the perpetuated racial violence that consigned so many Black children to poverty. In college, she also experienced her first crisis of faith as she realized that she had grown up with an image of Jesus as a white man. "How could a White Jesus ever care about me," she asked herself, "not to speak of caring for poor Black children? And how could I, a Black person, ever have faith in a White Jesus?"

It was Douglas's college chaplain, David Woodyard, who introduced her to the writings of Black liberation theologian **James Cone.** Cone's critique of white Christianity became a spiritual lifeline.

Here was someone within the church naming the horrific realities of white Christianity's complicity with

LEARN ABOUT IT

James Cone (1938–2018) was an American theologian best known as the founder of Black liberation theology. His groundbreaking works— *Black Theology and Black Power* and *A Black Theology of Liberation*— challenged traditional (white) Christian theology by centering the experiences of oppressed Black people and arguing that social justice was at the root of the gospel.

slavery and all its evils. Cone posited the liberating image of Jesus as the Black Christ, one in solidarity with oppressed people. "When I read Cone's words," Douglas recounts, "my questions were answered. I could be Black with a love for Jesus without contradiction, because in fact Jesus was Black like me. As Cone made clear, Jesus, born in poverty, was one with all those Black children who were trapped behind the life-draining color line of inner-city realities." Cone's theology gave Douglas renewed appreciation for the faith passed down to her. She would go on to expand the horizons of Black theology with a focus on the experience of Black women in white society and LGBTQ+ people in the Black church.

Douglas believes that Jesus, as the incarnation of God in human life, continues to experience the realities of crucifixion in the lives of Black people and feels the pain of it as if for the first time. She walks with him to the cross. But she also finds hope in his resurrection—the same hope that her forebears clung to and that she is determined to carry forth.

There is undeniably a sacrificial component in the decision to stay, a sense of loss for the roads not taken and the weight of burdens that we choose not to lay down. Staying can also be a loving gift to ourselves and others. For in choosing stability in one area of our lives, we give those who depend on us an opportunity to thrive and grow. We don't typically associate stability with sacrificial love, for there is nothing visibly heroic about it, but beneath the surface, there is another story to be told.

LEARN
ABOUT IT

Eleanor Roosevelt (1884–1962) redefined the role of First Lady. Before her, it was a ceremonial position, and under Roosevelt, it became a position of active political and social engagement. She championed human rights, women's rights, and social justice, using her platform to broadly advocate for the marginalized, cementing her legacy as a global humanitarian.

I HAVE ALWAYS BEEN FASCINATED with public marriages in which both partners share a vocation. That was especially true for the presidential couple who led our nation through the Great Depression and World War II— Franklin and **Eleanor Roosevelt**. In a time of unrest and suffering, Franklin and Eleanor were icons of stability, compassion, and courage. The country looked to both of them for strength, not knowing that there was a private side to this iconic marriage that never would have survived today's twenty-four-hour news cycle and social media. Very few knew that their marriage had nearly ended in divorce twenty years before they entered the White House. Given the circumstances and social expectations of their time and economic class, such a scandal would likely have derailed Franklin's political career long before he was a candidate for president. Eleanor chose to stay. It's impossible to imagine what the nation, and the world, would be like today had she chosen otherwise.

Eleanor had accepted the marriage proposal of her distant cousin Franklin when she was still a teenager. Franklin already had political ambitions, and Eleanor longed to be of service for good in the world. At the turn of the new century, each saw the world as at once perilous and full of promise. Soon, however, Eleanor's call to public service was submerged in the exhaustion of childbirth and parenting. Sara Roosevelt, Franklin's mother, was an overbearing presence in their household, and Eleanor assumed a subservient, almost childlike role as Franklin's career flourished.

Eleanor also refused to acknowledge what had become widely known in Washington's social circles: Franklin had fallen in love with her personal secretary, Lucy Mercer. The affair went on for years. Eleanor persisted in denial, at least publicly, until a fateful night in 1918 when Franklin returned home from an extended trip to Europe. Unpacking Franklin's bags, Eleanor discovered Lucy's love letters. Years later, in private correspondence, she acknowledged that "The bottom dropped out of my own particular world, and I faced myself, my surroundings, and my world, honestly for the first time."

While Eleanor's heart was broken, her mind was clear, and she immediately offered Franklin his freedom. Sara Roosevelt was mortified at the prospect of the spectacle of a divorce, and she threatened to cut off Franklin from the financial support of the family fortune upon which his privileged life and political future depended. In the chaotic days that followed, Franklin's closest friend and political adviser, Louis Howe, served as mediator. What began as a tentative conversation became a negotiation of marital terms. Sara was distraught, Franklin sulked, and Eleanor remained calm. She would not stay in a marriage where she was not wanted.

Although Franklin left no known public or private record of his true feelings, his biographers describe Lucy Mercer as the love of his life. Nonetheless, his love for politics and public service proved greater, and he broke off their relationship. He apologized to Eleanor and vowed never to see Lucy again. It was a promise he did not keep, but they were apart long enough for Franklin and Eleanor to find their way.

In choosing to stay, Eleanor redefined what it meant for her to be Franklin's wife. She insisted on separate bedrooms and having full authority over their household. She fired all the servants who were subservient to her mother-in-law and hired people loyal to her instead. Biographer Blanche Wiesen Cook writes, "As Eleanor waited for her heart to heal, a new resolve emerged, in the shape of words that were to be the banner of her adult life, words she repeated as advice to her many friends and the young people who would from then on enter her world, a new world of action and activism: 'The life you live is your own.'"

Indeed, Franklin would soon need Eleanor more than anyone could have predicted. In the summer of 1921, he contracted polio. In the first touch-and-go weeks of high fever and agonizing pain, Eleanor never left his side. As Franklin inched toward partial recovery and eventually came to terms with permanent paralysis, Eleanor and Howe were united in their determination to keep his aspirations alive. Eleanor realized that without a future in politics, Franklin would give up altogether. She believed in that future, and that she belonged beside him.

By the time Franklin was elected president in 1932, their outwardly focused marriage was firmly established, their partnership based not on intimacy but on shared values, mutual need, and affection. They also established their own communities of support—men and women who tended to their emotional and physical needs while they served the nation. Eleanor traveled on Franklin's behalf, spoke for him at events he could not attend, and returned with reports of what she had witnessed. She was his most trusted adviser. Franklin encouraged Eleanor's activism and defended her against detractors when she spoke out against racial injustice and abusive labor practices.

I have long pondered the cost and consequences of Eleanor's decision to stay. Yes, she would stay married, but not as before. She would be her husband's partner, but she also gave herself permission to seek happiness wherever she could find it. Most important, she determined what truly mattered to her, which was a life of service, committed to the ideals of justice, peace, and human rights. She prioritized showing up in racially integrated spaces and befriending those working for civil rights, including Howard Thurman. In 1944, she was the keynote speaker for his send-off when he left Washington, D.C., for San Francisco, and she was among the first to sign a commitment card for his interracial church.

Most decisions to stay are less widely consequential than Eleanor Roosevelt's or Kelly Brown Douglas's, but the impact of our choices may reach further than we will ever know. Choosing to stay is rarely recognized for the heroic journey it can be, and few may see the depth of crisis we experience as our lives hang in the balance. It is, by and large, an inner struggle. That may be for the best, for what we need most of all is time and space to reflect and a willingness to trust our inner compass. Even in situations that we desperately want to leave, we may well come to the astonishing realization that staying is our choice.

We are not trapped. We are agents of our destiny.

There is no manual to consult or blueprint to follow in these testing times. But there are paths of wisdom that come to us in literature and in our faith traditions. And we learn from the courage of others. Most important is the discerning of our hearts, for each of us must come to our own decision.

THINK
ABOUT IT

Earlier in the book, we looked at the fictional character Harry Potter as an example of deciding to go. Today, real people often find themselves facing a decision about staying when they think about the world of Harry Potter. Since 2020, author J. K. Rowling's repeated transphobic statements have led many longtime fans of the books and films to reconsider their personal engagement with the franchise. It is not an easy choice, and there is no one right answer. Many have chosen to go, but others continue to find wisdom and community in the stories and the fandom that transcend the author's personal beliefs. They choose to stay.

Whether or not we consciously call upon God, it is a holy journey. We are wrestling with profound questions of identity and relationship, the purpose of our lives, and the sacrificial nature of love. There is nothing passive or inconsequential in choosing to stay. With it paradoxically comes an invitation to start something new.

To that new beginning, we now turn.

Harry Potter actor Daniel Radcliffe attributes his own advocacy on behalf of LGBTQIA+ people to his personal connection to the stories. He says, "I did have a realization of a connection to Harry Potter and this stuff. A lot of people found some solace in those books and films who were dealing with feeling closeted or rejected by their family or living with a secret."

Have you ever decided to stay? What happened? Where in your life could benefit from deep intention and engagement?

CHAPTER THREE

DECIDING TO START

A journey of a thousand miles begins with a single step.
—Laozi, Dao De Jing

The call to start is almost always initially private. The first steps are typically small, and it often takes a moment to see where those first stirrings ultimately lead. Moreover, not every attempt we make results in a dramatic change. Sometimes we have to stay where we are for a time. Sometimes starting requires significant preparation. We might even go backward at first. Regardless, however we start, we can generally trace our beginnings to a moment that hardly anyone noticed.

For example, it is surprisingly easy to read all the biblical accounts of Jesus's life and miss one of his most decisive moments. Of the four Gospel writers, Matthew, Mark, Luke, and John, only Luke mentions it, almost in passing. Yet this is the moment when Jesus embarks on the journey leading to his death—and he knows it.

Previously, Jesus had stayed close to the villages in northern Israel surrounding a large lake known as the Sea of Galilee. His hometown of Nazareth served as base camp for his ministry of teaching, healing, and feeding the community alongside a small group of disciples, or students, who traveled with him.

One day Jesus takes a break from his ministry and climbs a nearby mountain. For Jesus, climbing mountains was a form of prayer. Hiking cleared his mind, and the views gave him perspective as he cast his gaze toward the horizon. It was his custom to slip away periodically for a night, even an entire day, to escape from the crowds that followed him everywhere. He typically went alone, but this time he invites three of his closest disciples—James, John, and Simon Peter—to join him.

On the mountaintop, Jesus has a mystical experience in the form of a conversation with his spiritual ancestors Moses and Elijah. His disciples watch as **a light comes upon him that seems to change his appearance**, and they hear the voice of God speak from a cloud: "This is my Son, my Chosen; listen to him!" For reasons they don't understand at the time, Jesus swears them to silence.

LEARN ABOUT IT

The Transfiguration is a moment in the Christian Bible where Jesus reveals his divinity to three of his closest disciples. It's a moment that is hard to grasp in our modern world, as Jesus's face "shines like the sun" and his clothes "became dazzlingly white"—but it isn't some clever trick. Instead, it's a moment of profound revelation that tells his friends to be ready for his coming suffering and resurrection.

A whirlwind of human need awaits Jesus when he comes down from the mountain. Before he has a chance to catch his breath, he's back at work. But something is different. Whatever Jesus experienced when the light shone and the voice from the cloud spoke, his ministry includes a new wrinkle. Namely, his coming death. As a result, Jesus makes the pivotal decision to go to Jerusalem, the city where all the prophets before him went to die.

In the seventy-eight-mile journey from Galilee to Jerusalem, Jesus's ministry looks much the same as before. He teaches and heals people. He tells some of his most memorable parables on the road, including the story of the Good Samaritan and the Prodigal Son. He makes a point of traveling to areas that most Jews avoided and speaking to the outcasts, telling them of God's generous, inclusive love. He has dinner with his close friends Martha, Mary, and Lazarus and honors Mary's choice to take her place among the men rather than busy herself in the kitchen. The **stories** are important, but perhaps not as important as the journey itself.

The only clue we're given that time is running out for him is his impatience with those still hesitating to join him, and the urgent way Jesus teaches his disciples along the way. He repeatedly tells them that

LEARN ABOUT IT

Jesus used parables, or short stories, to help listeners grasp deeper, theological concepts such as mercy, compassion, and the Kingdom of God. In both the Prodigal Son and the Good Samaritan parables, Jesus challenges typical social and moral understanding.

he will not be with them much longer—something they do their best to ignore.

Early in my years as a priest, a woman named Cindy Dowson told me she had decided to pursue her dream of becoming a nurse. This was a big deal because Cindy had never gone to college, and she hadn't done well in high school. When she was a teenager, Cindy's main objective was to live on her own. She waited tables at first and eventually landed an office job, where she stayed for fourteen years. She met and married her husband, Scott, and they started their family. It was after the birth of their third child and Cindy had left her job to care for their children full-time when she told me of her decision to start on the journey toward the job she had always wanted.

Starting meant taking one night class per semester at a local community college because she needed remedial and prerequisite courses before she could even apply to the nursing program. For six years, Cindy worked slowly and steadily. When at last she was accepted into the nursing program, she enrolled full-time for two more years. Each day, she would rise early to study several hours before her children woke up and then return to her studies after they fell asleep at night.

Each decision to start a courageous journey is unique, yet the experience is universal. For example, when did you learn to walk or to speak? The first stirrings are instinctive and unconscious. Still, there is agency in the decision to pull yourself up and take those first steps toward outstretched arms. As you grow, things such as learning to ride a bicycle or playing a musical instrument require a choice. It's in this choice that we see even more clearly the courage required in a person's decision to start. There is risk and vulnerability in learning something new, and excitement at accomplishing what was once impossible.

Humans are not the only species with the capacity to begin journeys of consequence. My bird-watching husband tells me of certain species that make migratory treks from one end of a continent to another. How do birds know when to start? What keeps them on course when they've not made the journey before? Where humans differ is in our capacity to envision possibilities beyond our sight and move toward them. It isn't instinct alone. Even though we make the choice, we often feel a spiritual beckoning that summons us toward a certain destiny—a certain decision. When we make that decision, the path ahead may be clear, as in a college major or career path. Others are ambiguous, more like driving at night in the fog. In either case, whatever lies beyond the horizon can be realized only by moving toward it.

One of my formative decisions to start came to me by surprise. I had no definitive destination or path, and surely no guaranteed outcomes, but I realized that if I ever wanted to be considered for a position of greater influence in the church or beyond, I needed to be ready when the opportunity presented itself. I wasn't sure how to go about it, only that it was critical to begin.

Part of my story involves the stories of others. Ernesto Medina attended a conference I led in June 2003. At the time, he was serving as the provost of the Episcopal Cathedral in Los Angeles.

Throughout the week, Ernesto dazzled us with his creativity and exuberant spirit. He gently teased me for my serious demeanor and invited me to kick back and have fun with the group. When it was Ernesto's turn to speak on the last day, he said, "I want to dance at my grandchild's wedding." It was a vision of joy, characteristic of his seemingly boundless jubilance, yet something in his voice caught my attention. Ernesto was exactly my age, and like me, he had two adolescent children. Grandchildren were a long way off for both of us. "Life expectancy for men like me isn't great," he said quietly. "Taking care of myself physically is a struggle. Just before I came to this conference, I was diagnosed with diabetes." He paused. "I want to do whatever it takes to be there for my kids and my grandkids."

Ruthanna Hooke was at that same conference. She had recently been hired as a professor at Virginia Theological Seminary, where I studied for my doctorate of ministry. She was also the first partnered LGBTQ+ person to serve on the faculty. In accepting her position, Ruthanna found herself at the center of **our church's human sexuality debates**, which at the time were often polarizing and mean-spirited. She did not relish the spotlight focused on her private life. Her call was to teach.

During our week together, Ruthanna allowed herself to imagine a future in which she would not be known primarily for her sexual orientation. When the time came to speak of her aspirations, she said, "I want to be recognized as the top of my field within ten years." There was a spark of determination, even defiance, in her eyes. I wanted to stand and applaud.

I have carried Ernesto and Ruthanna in my heart for more than twenty years. Their words became my own as I savored watching our sons grow up and imagined the grandmother I would be to their future children. I allowed myself to acknowledge my own ambition to be a leader, with the ability to make a real difference in people's lives and the direction of our country. Ernesto and Ruthanna helped me remember that such aspirations require daily intentionality over long periods of time. I needed to start and keep moving toward my future.

As all this was stirring in my personal life, I was asked to serve on a leadership team, known as the Bishop's Commission for Mission Strategy. We gathered information on the state of our church and tried to make sense of it. We held listening sessions to better

LEARN ABOUT IT

The ordination of the first openly gay bishop, Gene Robinson, which occurred in 2003, sparked both celebration and controversy in the Episcopal Church and beyond. Still, even though the Episcopal Church has a long history of including LGBTQ+ individuals, there remains work to do. Despite differences, the Episcopal Church's record of inclusion continues to develop, but is always rooted in the truth that God loves us all—no exceptions.

understand the lived experience of our people. We pored over data that told a story of rapid decline in the health of the church as an institution. We often argued among ourselves and were quick to point out the failings of others. A consultant of our group, Dr. Craig Van Gelder, gently invited us to look at our own behavior and move beyond what he called "our culture of critique."

"It takes no energy or creativity to point out what's wrong," he said. "But for everything you criticize, I challenge you to offer at least one suggestion for making it better."

His words have stayed with me as an invaluable reminder that although it is easy to find fault, the people who make a difference for good are those who work for creative solutions.

During that work, we came to the sobering conclusion that the future of our diocese, and the Episcopal Church in general, was bleak, given how many congregations were struggling simply to survive. Dr. Van Gelder observed that we lacked a coherent vision or a unifying sense of identity or purpose. The implications weighed heavily on my heart. During a break, I took a walk with my friend and colleague the Reverend Michele Morgan. Her path to ordination as a priest, as well as finding work in the church, had been anything but easy even with the Episcopal Church's movement toward full inclusion of LGBTQ+ people.

I confided to Michele that I wasn't even sure that it mattered to God if the Episcopal Church survived. The mission of Jesus and the work of the Holy Spirit was not in question, only the relevance of our church in that work. Even if we did survive, to whom would it matter?

Michele was quiet for a moment and then said, "It matters to me. This is the church that welcomed me."

Her words went straight to my heart, and I thought of all the other people I loved who had found a spiritual home in my church and throughout our denomination.

I realized that I was not going to give up on our church.

That was the day I said to God that if I were ever called to be bishop, I would give my whole heart to the work. I knew it was what I wanted to do, and like Ruthanna, I dared to name my ambition. Our bishop announced his decision to retire later that year, and when the time came, I put my name forward to be among the candidates from which his successor would be elected. It would be two years before the convention in which delegates from around the diocese **chose the next bishop**.

I continued working at my church while preparing for what I hoped and believed would be my future. Looking back, I see more clearly what I couldn't acknowledge at the time—that I was not universally loved or respected among my peers, nor did many people

LEARN
ABOUT IT

The name *Episcopal* is derived from the Greek word *episcopos*, which means "bishop" or "overseer." It's a nod to the leadership structure of the Episcopal Church, which is governed by bishops, who play a key role in both the leadership and the administration of the church itself.

trust my motives. For all my preparation and sense of call, there was a quiet anxiety in the air on the day of the election among my supporters that I tried to ignore. By the end of the second round of votes, it was clear that I would not be elected.

In the weeks and months that followed, I felt my world grow small. Our sons were off at college. My husband's work kept him busy. The ministry at St. John's Episcopal Church in Minneapolis carried on. I went through the motions of living, knowing full well that the church deserved more from me than I could give. When I finally told the church leaders that I didn't have a guiding vision to lead them anymore, a wise and caring woman, Kay Kramer, gently asked, "Do you have sufficient vision for a year?" I thought for a moment and answered honestly that I did. She smiled. "Then why don't we take things one year at a time for now?" I felt her blessing to lead as best I could for a window of time.

But what was I to do with all the signs and aspirations that had led me to consider a more influential position? It physically hurt to remember how much I had wanted to be elected bishop and at the same time how embarrassing it was to acknowledge that desire. Yet again, I was driving in the fog, unable to see past my headlights.

A haunting line from a poem called "Sweet Darkness" by David Whyte guided me in that year when the future went dark.

> *Give up all the other worlds*
> *except the one to which you belong.*

On the day the new bishop was ordained to his post, I took part in the service alongside my clergy colleagues. Waiting for me at home that afternoon was an email from a friend, Lisa Kimball, who had recently moved to join the faculty of Virginia Theological Seminary. On that same day, she told me, the bishop of the Episcopal Diocese of Washington had announced his retirement.

"Consider this," is all she wrote.

At the time, nothing felt more unlikely than being elected bishop anywhere, much less in Washington, D.C. Yet undeniably, I felt a spark of hope, and with it, in time, permission to dream again.

I didn't say a word to anyone.

It's tempting to view the decisions and events of those years as all leading to where I am now, but as I lived them, the path was anything but certain. I could only see far enough to take the next step, and the next, and then the next.

The disappointments I'd experienced caused me to doubt my inner drive, and I tried to imagine other paths I could take to live a meaningful life. Somewhere during the two-year journey from the day I first learned that the former bishop of Washington was retiring to the day of my election to that post, I came to accept two realities: first, that the call to dedicate my life to the renewal and structural transformation of the Episcopal Church was not one I could ignore or negotiate, and second, that I could not know in advance the context in which I would heed that call. The time had come for me to leave, and should no diocese choose me as their bishop, then I would have to find another way.

<hr>

HISTORY IS FULL OF STORIES, often told from the perspective of successful outcomes, that gloss over the prolonged struggle that follows a decision to start down such a path, and how often those in one generation take the vision as far as they can and then must pass it on to the next. Sometimes the next generation even undoes the hard-won accomplishments of their forebears with the pendulum swings such as we are witnessing in our time with the overturning of Roe v. Wade and other U.S. Supreme Court decisions. In history, as in our personal lives, there is no straight path.

Yet only when brave individuals choose to start and then persevere does society change.

Supreme Court Justice Thurgood Marshall's relentless quest across decades to challenge Jim Crow laws and flagrant lynching practices is one such example. Marshall's tenacity and legal genius are widely known from the Brown v. Board of Education Supreme Court decision of 1954, which declared segregated schools unconstitutional. Faded from our collective memory is how hard he worked before Brown v. Board to eradicate the evils of segregation, winning the grudging respect of white judges and attorneys across the South and attaining near-godlike status in Black communities.

Marshall came from a proud lineage of enslaved and free Black people who fought against slavery, established businesses, educated their children during Reconstruction, and built homes in the newly integrated neighborhoods of Baltimore. But by the time Thurgood was born in 1908, the resurgence of white supremacist laws and policies was well under way. During his childhood and adolescence, increasingly oppressive restrictions stripped Black Americans of their legal rights and access to equal housing, employment opportunities, and education. Lynching—the murder of Black people by vigilantes, often with the silent approval of white police—became the means of social control.

LEARN
ABOUT IT

Thurgood Marshall was the first African American Supreme Court Justice and became the lead attorney for the National Association for the Advancement of Colored Persons (NAACP). One of Marshall's most important achievements was the 1954 Supreme Court case Brown v. Board of Education, which made segregation in public schools unconstitutional. He was appointed to the Supreme Court in 1967, serving until his retirement in 1991.

Marshall's family protected their children as best they could from the violence and cruelty of segregation, sending them to the best schools they could afford and drawing upon the resources of extended family to help them attain college educations. Still, Marshall and his classmates were keenly aware that the dominant society treated them as less worthy of educational investment than their white counterparts.

His political awakening began in high school, when the

principal punished him for misbehavior by giving him a copy of the U.S. Constitution and telling him to memorize it, which he did in one afternoon. His interest slowly grew while he attended Lincoln University, a historically Black university in Pennsylvania. When he was denied admission to the University of Maryland School of Law on the basis of race, he reluctantly applied to Howard University School of Law, which he considered a far less reputable institution.

Marshall had the extraordinarily good fortune to arrive at Howard in 1930, the same year as its new dean, Charles Hamilton Houston. The dean's determination to raise a generation of brilliant Black lawyers inspired Marshall. Under Houston's commanding leadership, Marshall began his lifelong journey to use the legal system to dismantle Jim Crow.

One decisive moment to start on the long road to justice came during his last year at Howard. Dean Houston had invited Marshall to join his legal defense team in the case of a Black man from Virginia, George Crawford, accused of murdering two white women. Together they worked for months on Crawford's defense. Despite the lack of a weapon or witnesses linking Crawford to the crime, the all-white jury found him guilty. Yet because of the tenacity of his defense team, Crawford escaped the death penalty, which was cause for celebration. As Marshall would say later, "If you get a life term for a Negro charged with killing a white person in Virginia, you've won, because normally they were hanging them."

The Crawford case, and the opportunity while still in his early twenties to be in the courtroom alongside his brilliant mentor, set Marshall on a course from which he never wavered. Houston often told his students that they could become the architects not only of a more just legal system but a new social order, one court case at a time. That became Marshall's purpose in life.

Like other Black leaders of his generation, Marshall believed that he stood at the threshold of historical change, yet he held no illusions about the daunting task before him. His tenacity and legal brilliance were evident in his arguments before the Supreme Court, and then as the first Black American to serve on the court from 1967 to 1991.

Unlike other civil rights champions of his time, Marshall lived long enough to witness the tides of change turn once again, this time against his efforts. He grew increasingly isolated on the Supreme Court, relegated to writing dissenting opinions in case after case. In his final years, he became a recluse. Yet his legacy remains among the finest of his peers, born of his unwavering conviction that the U.S. Constitution, although not written for his people, could provide the path for their freedom; that courts of law, although often unjustly biased against them, could be the arena of

LEARN ABOUT IT

The Constitution did not originally grant either citizenship or basic rights to enslaved Black people. Clauses such as the Three-Fifths Compromise (which described how enslaved people would be counted as "three-fifths" of a person for the purpose of representation and taxes) and other parts of the text protected and enforced the institution of slavery. The passage of the Thirteenth, Fourteenth, and Fifteenth Amendments after the Civil War was the start of repairing these injustices.

justice; and that just laws could, in fact, encourage basic decency.

The Reverend Dr. Pauli Murray, a contemporary of Marshall's, also chose law as the best way to pursue justice for Black Americans. From an early age, she had been engaged in nearly every form of advocacy and agitation, most notably with her favorite form of protest: "confrontation by typewriter." She was determined, unlike most men of her generation, including Thurgood Marshall, to include Black women in the struggle for equal rights.

Murray's life consisted of one decisive moment after another. Her mixed-race family was a source of pride and devotion, yet mental illness and poverty loomed large. She was raised by her aunt Pauline, a teacher who encouraged her to pursue education, and despite the formidable barriers, Murray spent much of her life in academic settings, consistently at the top of the class. She was always poor, working for almost no pay as a writer, union organizer, and fundraiser, and later as an attorney. She struggled privately with her sexuality and gender identity until she met the love of her life, Irene Barlow, in her late forties. Murray's legal arguments are now part of the canon of civil rights law, yet she was never adequately compensated or recognized for her efforts.

Murray entered Howard Law School in 1941, a little over a decade after Thurgood Marshall. As she prepared to take her place among the aspiring lawyers at Howard, Pauli was stunned by the overwhelming gender prejudice she encountered. She had grown up surrounded by strong women, attended a women's college, been befriended by Eleanor Roosevelt, and worked in organizations where women held positions of leadership. This was the first time she experienced the full-on effects of gender discrimination.

"The racial factor was removed in the intimate environment of a Negro law school dominated by men," she wrote in her memoir, "and the factor of gender was fully exposed."

All of her energies had previously been focused on the struggle against prejudicial laws based on race. Now in a nearly all-male Black institution she encountered what she described as the twin evils of discriminatory violence that she aptly called "Jane Crow." That marginalization galvanized her. It became her lifelong quest to treat both race and gender equity as nonnegotiable in civil rights law and societal practice.

Murray's classmates and professors

LEARN ABOUT IT

The Reverend Dr. Pauli Murray (1910–1985) was a priest, lawyer, poet, and relentless advocate for civil rights and gender equality. Murray was a cofounder of the National Organization for Women (NOW) and the first African American woman to be ordained an Episcopal priest. Her groundbreaking work challenged the intersections of racial and gender discrimination and laid the groundwork for future equality movements.

initially scoffed at the notion that women should be included in the legal struggle for civil rights. Her direct attack on Plessy v. Ferguson—a notorious 1896 U.S. Supreme Court decision that upheld the constitutionality of racial segregation laws—became the foundation for later writings that would one day garner the attention of Howard Thurman and, later, Ruth Bader Ginsburg. Murray's comprehensive study on racial segregation laws throughout the South, *States' Laws on Race and Color: Studies in the Legal History of the South*, became, in Thurgood Marshall's words, "the 'Bible' for civil rights litigators." She also consistently called male leaders to account and joined forces with the burgeoning women's movement.

Murray is a case study of a life lived ahead of its time. She laid the foundations for what became typical in our society. Although her personal experience was often one of failure, she took satisfaction when her ideals were vindicated. In her later years, she often said, "I have lived to see my lost causes found."

One of her delayed victories has special significance for me and all women clergy: As a practicing Christian and lifelong member of the Episcopal Church, Murray actively participated in the decades-long debate over whether to allow women to serve as priests. In the microcosm of the church, it was as fierce and nasty a debate as the struggle for women's rights in the wider society. In 1977, the governing body of the Episcopal Church voted for that historic change, and Pauli Murray became the first Black woman to be ordained as an Episcopal priest.

A VISION OF WHAT COULD BE is what inspires us to start on a journey. Sometimes we move decisively toward a goal; other times we begin only with a subtle movement. In either case, the road is long and there are no shortcuts. We begin by taking the first step, and every step that follows.

Along the way we are changed, the goal itself may change, or perhaps it may not even be realized. But in deciding to start, we put ourselves on the path of our transformation. The vision may be audacious, but along with it comes a sense of excitement and purpose. In the inevitable moments of disappointment and failure, we learn to be brave and not give up.

Deciding to start on a courageous journey has the effect of weaving our past experiences into a larger tapestry of meaning. Nothing is lost or wasted. We recognize that our efforts are beholden to those who went before us. From their perspective, our decision to start may, in fact, be a continuation of the work that they began, or the realization in our lifetimes of what they could only imagine in their dreams. When we decide to start toward something that requires courage, we are often creating new possibilities for those who come after us. Our example may be the one to inspire others to turn toward their Jerusalem, whatever the path God has set before them.

There are, however, no guarantees when we start that we will reach the shore beckoning on our horizon. There are forces in life and in our world that stall and prevent forward movement, failures from which we cannot recover, and circumstances beyond our control and beyond our power to change that call for a different order of courage, its own new start.

CHAPTER FOUR

ACCEPTING WHAT YOU DO NOT CHOOSE

God, grant me the serenity to accept the things I cannot change, the courage to change the things I can, and the wisdom to know the difference.
—Reinhold Niebuhr

The news didn't come as a complete surprise. My sister had known for months that something wasn't right. But when Christine called early on a January morning to tell me that her life partner, Jack, had been diagnosed with stage IV lung cancer, her voice was still filled with shock and dread.

Jack immediately began treatment. The side effects were awful. Christine's life, once filled with her grandchildren's activities, volunteer work, and helping out at Jack's business, was now entirely centered on his care. One day Christine told me that she now knew every corner of the hospital complex, from the lower levels of the parking garage, through the labyrinthine hallways, and on to numerous floors.

"It wasn't in my plan for 2019," she said, laughing wryly, "but I guess this is what God wanted me to learn."

I knew Christine didn't really believe that God had orchestrated Jack's illness so she might acquire this ordinary bit of information. It was her way of expressing how she was coming to terms with an awful situation, trusting that God was somewhere in the mess of it all. I had always admired my sister for her strength and do-what-has-to-be-done approach to life; now I watched in awe as she cared for Jack with determined love.

Jack was declared cancer-free, but the good news came with sober advice. Because the cancer could return, it was time for him to get his affairs in order and do everything on his bucket list. Christine went into high gear. She encouraged Jack's brothers to take him on a Gulf Coast fishing expedition, his great passion. She ensured that he spent time with his children and grandchildren, and she finalized the transfer of his business to one of his daughters. That summer, they visited Yellowstone National Park, a dream vacation clouded by Jack's growing fatigue.

When they returned from Yellowstone, the doctors confirmed that the tumors had returned and spread. Jack's options were diminishing, yet he remained determined to fight, and Christine quietly supported him. In conversations with me, however, she expressed sadness at how he was choosing to spend his last days. She had to hold back her anger at his doctors. Why were they giving him false hope?

When my husband and I went to see Jack, a shadow of his former self, he greeted us warmly. Christine looked exhausted, but she took him to treatment every day, after which he would sleep. In the late afternoons, we sat on the back porch and I asked if he was afraid. "It doesn't look good," he acknowledged, but said no more. When the time came to say goodbye, Jack thanked us for coming. "I look forward to seeing you again," he said. On the day we returned home, his doctors told Jack there was nothing more they could do. Before Christine had time to set up the hospital bed she had ordered, he passed away.

Watching Christine navigate Jack's illness and care, I was reminded of Howard Thurman's words about the spiritual strength required to accept an unchosen fate as one's destiny, and the grace that comes from that acceptance. Among the many things Christine had to make peace with was Jack's inability to accept what he could not change, and a health-care system unwilling to let him die in peace. The only thing within her control was how she would respond.

She chose love.

Accepting what we do not choose and cannot change is one of the most courageous decisions we make—and also the most difficult. When faced with a terrible situation, denial is often our first

LEARN
ABOUT IT

The Serenity Prayer, which opens this chapter, is a short prayer that's attributed to American theologian Reinhold Niebuhr. It's a simple yet profound statement that acknowledges the limitations of our control while emphasizing the importance of discernment and action when and where possible.

response as our brains struggle to take in an unwanted new reality. When the facts stubbornly persist, we do whatever we can to avert the outcome we most dread. This is instinctual, for we were created for life. Even **the Serenity Prayer**, with its emphasis on accepting the things we cannot change, also exhorts us to change the things we can. But we generally don't get to acceptance until we've exhausted all other options.

Acceptance can look like passivity or resignation, but it's not. When we accept something beyond our control, we actively engage with whatever we're faced with, precisely because it is what we're faced with. There's no turning away and no turning back. I once experienced severe air turbulence, the kind that made us all wonder if the airplane was going down. When the captain came over the loudspeaker during the worst of it, he conveyed both gravity and calmness: "Folks, as you can tell, we've hit a rough patch. I'm sorry to say that there's no getting around it—so hold on tight. The only way out of this one is through."

As someone who speaks about God nearly every Sunday, I've learned that one of the most important functions of preaching is to name reality as best I can. That task was especially clear to me on March 8, 2020, after we had abruptly closed all Episcopal churches in the Diocese of Washington. This was in the early days of the COVID-19 pandemic, when closing our churches felt like the most drastic decision I would ever make as bishop. Little did we know how many more dramatic decisions would follow as the pandemic came to dominate our lives.

I realized that my task was to say what no one wanted to hear: It was time to brace ourselves for a long stretch of hardship and uncertainty. The refrain from an old hymn kept running through my mind: "Grant us wisdom, grant us courage, for the facing of this hour." Then I remembered young Frodo Baggins, the reluctant hero of **J. R. R. Tolkien**'s Lord of the Rings, and his acceptance of a fate he did not want.

In Tolkien's fictional land of wizards, elves, and gentle creatures known as hobbits, evil looms on the horizon. A dark lord named Sauron seeks to dominate and enslave all inhabitants of Middle-earth. The power he needs is contained in a magic ring that has been lost for centuries, until a hobbit named Bilbo finds it and gives it to his nephew, Frodo. The wise wizard Gandalf knows both the history of the ring and

LEARN ABOUT IT

J. R. R. Tolkien was a devout Roman Catholic, and his faith permeated his life and literary works. While he was explicit that his stories were not allegories, his Catholic faith profoundly influenced the themes of good versus evil, free will, and the importance of humility and grace that run through his novels.

the necessity of preventing it from falling into Sauron's hands. He believes that Frodo is the one destined to carry the ring to the only place it can be destroyed, a fiery volcano in the land of Mordor known as Mount Doom.

In an exchange that has inspired readers for generations, Gandalf exhorts Frodo to have courage:

"The ring came to you for a reason," Gandalf tells him. "There is comfort in that."

"I wish the ring had never come to me," Frodo says. "I wish this had never happened."

"So do all who live in such times," Gandalf replies. "But while we cannot choose the times we live in, we can choose how to respond to the time we are given."

At last, Frodo says, "I will take the ring, but I do not know the way."

Gandalf later assures him, "There are other forces at work in this world, Frodo, besides the will of evil."

I recounted that exchange the day we closed our churches, allowing Frodo to give voice to our collective wish that the pandemic had never happened. Yet in our time it came—not the first pandemic, nor the last. The story our children and grandchildren will want us to tell someday is not that we lived through the COVID pandemic, but how we did and what we learned. I wanted to convey that most bold of faith statements: There are forces for good at work in the world, even in the darkest hours. We are our best selves when we join those forces and do our part, tipping the scales ever more slightly toward the good.

As we made our way through 2020, COVID-19 laid bare the fault lines of our society, including racial and socioeconomic inequities, a weak public health-care system, and political polarization. As disproportionate death rates among people of color and instances of police and vigilante violence against Black Americans dominated the news, some began to speak of two interrelated pandemics: the coronavirus and systemic racism.

Two years into the pandemic, after the summer of protests sparked by the police murder of George Floyd, the tumultuous presidential election of 2020, and the violent insurrection at the U.S. Capitol on January 6, 2021, I was invited to lead a seminar on the challenges communities and organizations face when they can no longer rely on what served them well in the past—when they instead must make an evolutionary leap to thrive in a new environment.

Near the end of a day, one of the seminar faculty—a Jewish man raised in the shadow of the Holocaust—asked how I would respond to those wondering if the time had come to leave this country, for fear of the direction it was taking. I had the sense he was asking for himself, as well as others. Choosing my words carefully, I replied, "In crucible moments, everyone must make difficult decisions. Sometimes the wisest, most life-affirming decision is to leave because personal safety is not a given, nor is justice assured

LEARN
ABOUT IT

Dietrich Bonhoeffer was a German pastor, theologian, and anti-Nazi activist. His theological works, *The Cost of Discipleship* and *Life Together*, unpack themes of Christian discipleship and community. His theological commitments forced him into the resistance movement against Adolf Hitler and ultimately resulted in his imprisonment and execution.

in our criminal justice system. But this country needs leaders now, and citizens who can face things as they are, work to change what can be changed, and not give up hope for the future."

As I spoke, **Dietrich Bonhoeffer**, the German pastor and theologian who lived during the rise of Adolf Hitler, came to mind. Although most German Christian leaders in the 1930s and early '40s aligned themselves with a pro-Nazi German Christian movement, Bonhoeffer joined a resistance group known as the Confessing Church. When Bonhoeffer traveled to Great Britain and the United States to seek support from Christian leaders among the Allied nations, his friends and colleagues urged him to remain in exile, yet he chose to return to Germany. In a letter to Reinhold Niebuhr, a theologian and ethicist at Union Theological Seminary in New York, he explained why: "I will have no right to participate in the reconstruction of Christian life in Germany after the war if I do not share in the trials of this time with my people."

Bonhoeffer knew that his decision put his life in danger, and he was arrested in 1943 and executed by the Gestapo on April 9, 1945. "No one person is responsible for all the world's injustice and suffering," Bonhoeffer wrote from prison in 1943. "Still we must take part in Christ's greatness of heart, in the responsible action that in freedom lays hold of the hour. What remains is on the very narrow path, sometimes barely discernible, of taking each day as if it were the last and yet living it faithfully and responsibly as if there were yet again to be a great future."

Accepting what we do not choose invariably means making peace with suffering, a theme that runs through both the Jewish and Christian texts of the Bible. For the apostle Paul, author of most of the letters in the New Testament, suffering was a means of solidarity with Christ, whose message he had originally rejected. A Jewish leader in his own right, Paul never knew Jesus of Nazareth, and before his conversion experience, he persecuted Jesus's followers to eradicate what he considered a dangerous sect. But after his spiritual encounter with the Resurrected Christ and a period of self-imposed isolation, Paul emerged as a tireless evangelist and community organizer who almost single-handedly spread Jesus's message throughout the Roman Empire.

Paul believed that suffering was necessary. In his letter to the Romans, he goes so far as to say that followers of Jesus should boast in their suffering, knowing that suffering produces endurance, and endurance produces character, and character produces hope, and hope does not disappoint us, because God's love has been poured into our hearts through the Holy Spirit that has been given to us.

Paul wasn't masochistic. He was persuaded that God's love for humankind found its fullest expression in Jesus's crucifixion. As a follower of a crucified Lord, he felt called to take his share of suffering for love's sake. Paul didn't dwell on the hardships he endured for his efforts to make Christ known. In fact, he often wrote letters embracing and rejoicing in his suffering.

Only once did Paul give a glimpse into his inner struggle, and how he came to accept what he did not choose. In his second letter to the Christians in the city of Corinth, Paul referred to a "thorn in the flesh" that he believed was given to him "to keep him from being too elated."

Paul does not disclose the nature or source of his pain, only that it was always with him. His prayers that he be spared his suffering were answered, not in its release, but by the grace that allowed him to find meaning in it.

WE ALL HAVE MOMENTS OF CHALLENGE AND GRACE, learning to live with what we cannot change, the thorn we cannot remove. For me, it is chronic pain. To help with the pain, I consulted with all manner of specialists and underwent multiple tests, with no answers. I saw several chiropractors, each offering relief that never lasted more than a few hours. In desperation, I signed up for Rolfing sessions, a type of deep tissue manipulation that aims to relieve tension, and is known equally for its discomfort and its expense. During my last visit, the Rolfer told me that nothing was wrong with my back. "Your brain is caught in a pain loop," he said with authority. "The only thing you can do is to keep telling yourself that there's nothing wrong. Eventually your brain will get the message." For a while I believed him and tried to retrain my brain, but it didn't work. In fact, nothing "worked" in that I live with chronic back pain to this day.

In time, I found partial relief through a combination of exercise, periodic chiropractic treatment, posture improvement, and meditation. But first I had to accept the fact that the pain wasn't going away. I found another chiropractor who took my suffering seriously, and I saw him weekly for about six months. Eventually, he told me we'd done all we could do to correct my back issues. My heart sank.

"So it's never going to improve?" I asked.

"Probably not," he said. "But this may be one of those conditions that paradoxically promotes health."

Then he said something that has become a mantra for my life.

"If you tend to the weakness of your back, and surround it with strength, you will live a long and healthy life."

His words have proved true. Every morning I wake up with an aching back; every morning I take the necessary time to stretch my muscles until the pain lessens. At the end of the day, I stretch again so that I can sleep through the night. I've learned that if I want to live without constant discomfort, these exercises aren't optional, and over the years they have had the auxiliary effect of keeping my body flexible and relatively fit. If the pain becomes too distracting, as it sometimes does, there are a few other remedies, but I've long since given up the notion that I will ever be without it.

Acceptance is liberating, in that I no longer fight with my body, which allows my brain to focus on other things. Perhaps that was what the Rolfer was trying to tell me. Living with pain also has given me empathy for others who suffer from chronic illness and all the other circumstances we would never choose for ourselves but must learn to accept.

Acceptance, unlike avoidance or denial, never looks away from suffering but rather faces it directly and seeks to place it within a larger narrative. Dr. Rachel Naomi Remen, one of the earliest practitioners of integrative medicine, or mind/body health, has lived for more than sixty years with Crohn's disease—a chronic, progressive, and at times excruciatingly painful intestinal condition. Remen writes of a time when, after major abdominal surgery, she developed peritonitis, a life-threatening inflammation of the membrane lining the abdominal wall, along with sepsis, an equally grave condition. She was rushed back for further surgery. When the nurses came to change her bandages the next day, Remen looked down at her body, expecting to see a long incision held together with stitches. Instead, there was a gaping hole, as if she were still in the operating room. Because of her infections, the wound would be left open to heal on its own.

Remen couldn't bring herself to look at her abdomen again.

When the nurses came in each day to change the dressings, she turned her head, unable to face what she was certain was a mortal wound. This went on until it dawned on her that, in fact, she wasn't dying. When she looked again, Remen was astounded to see that the wound had begun to heal.

Yet not every wound heals, and there are illnesses with which we cannot live for long. Remen is no stranger to the limitations of the human body. In those instances, she stresses the importance of allowing grief to surface. Rising from that grief, she assures us, new possibilities emerge, and when cures are not possible, there can be healing of a different order. This isn't an answer we can hear when we are still holding on to a hope for recovery. Yet when that hope is gone, some among us attest to feeling alive in a new way. In a collection of essays titled *My Grandfather's Blessings: Stories of Strength, Refuge, and Belonging*, Remen writes, "As a physician, I have accompanied people as they have discovered in themselves an unexpected strength, a courage beyond what they would have thought possible, an unsuspected sense of compassion or a capacity for love deeper than they had ever dreamed." I think that is what Jesus meant when he likened the Kingdom of God within us to a pearl of great price.

IN THE CHRISTIAN FAITH, we see in Jesus the presence of God in human form, accepting the world as it is and revealing to us the nature of divine love. We can take solace from the fact that even Jesus struggled, and at the final hour prayed for deliverance from the pain and suffering of death.

According to three of the four Gospels—Mark, Matthew, and Luke—on the night before his death, Jesus shares a Passover meal with his twelve disciples and then retreats to a garden to pray. His closest disciples follow him there, but as the night wears on, sleep overtakes them, and Jesus is essentially alone. He prays these heart-breaking words: "Father, if it be possible, let this cup pass from me; yet not what I want, but what you want."

For all the clarity he once felt about his vocation and the initial acceptance of his fate, on that last night, Jesus prays to God that he be spared. This poignant scene assures us of his full humanity—that he, too, knew fear and the desire to live. We aren't told how long Jesus struggled between his appeal to God and coming to re-newed acceptance of what lay ahead. We only know that at some point during that long, lonely night, Jesus embraced his fate and made it an offering of sacrificial love.

Throughout his life and most especially in death, God re-vealed in Jesus the power of what Dr. Martin Luther King Jr. called **"redemptive suffering,"** a mystical, and admittedly controversial, assertion that undeserved suffering has spiritual power beyond our understanding or experience. For Christians, the crucified Jesus would become an icon of all human suffering, and his resurrection an eternal promise that pain and death will not have the final word.

The notion that suffering can wrest good from evil is developed throughout the Bible.

Particularly influential for the early Christian interpretation of Jesus's death are a series of poetic passages from the Jewish prophetic writings known as the Songs of the Suffering Servant. Found in the book of Isaiah, the poems describe a person of gentle spirit who was despised for his goodness. God chooses this servant for a mission of reconciliation and healing.

In Judaism, the Suffering Servant is understood as the nation of Israel, called to embrace the trials of exile and discover in the collective pain of its people a path of redemption for all nations. For early Christians, the Suffering Servant became the interpretative lens through which to grasp the meaning of Jesus's death on a cross.

LEARN ABOUT IT

Martin Luther King Jr.'s concept of redemptive suffering argues that unearned suffering is a powerful force for social transformation. He believed that by nonviolently enduring the pain inflicted by injustice, individuals could expose the moral bankruptcy of their oppressors and awaken the conscience of society. This philosophy wasn't about passively accepting suffering but rather about actively transforming it into a catalyst for positive change.

Our spiritual forebears struggled, as we do today, with the question that has no satisfactory answer: Why must we suffer? Efforts to explain why the Servant had to suffer and Jesus had to die an agonizing death abound in the biblical texts. As with our own attempts to find answers for our pain, the reasoning can be unsettling and even offensive. At one point, the writer of the Book of Isaiah in the Christian and Hebrew Bibles suggests that God has intentionally hurt the Servant: "Yet it was the will of the Lord to crush him with pain. . . . The righteous one, my servant, shall make many righteous, and he shall bear their iniquities."

It is a troubling view of God when compared with images and words that describe God as full of mercy and love. However, even the earliest followers of Jesus understood sacrifice, rooted in the idea that God's "justice" has no choice but to demand payment for the sins of humankind. Another way it is described is that Jesus's sacrifice and death on the cross is an expression of how far God will go to love us.

I have struggled with this view of God and Jesus for most of my life of faith. I am not alone. For Christians and non-Christians alike, this view of Jesus's suffering is the most challenging and, frankly, unappealing aspect of our tradition. It doesn't help us answer the arguably big question of why the innocent suffer, either, leaving us instead with a God who requires payment for human sin.

This doesn't mean I don't recognize my personal need for a saving grace that is greater than my sinfulness or that I don't believe Jesus died for the sins of the world. Still, atonement theory remains at best an incomplete understanding of Jesus's redemptive suffering. It suggests that his death was a kind of trade, a transaction between God and Jesus alone. The late Christian writer Rachel Held Evans said it best: "Jesus did not simply die to save us from our sins; Jesus lived to save us from our sins. His life and teachings show us the way to liberation." Jesus approached his death trusting in God's love despite what he had to endure.

The earliest Christians knew beyond a shadow of a doubt that Jesus's way was one of **sacrificial love**. It also provides a window into God's heart. In Jesus's life, death, and resurrection, we see the human face of God, as one who suffers alongside humankind to reveal the depth of divine love. Those called to follow him are to walk on that same path of love, taking up our own cross as life demands.

Admittedly, when faced with evil and suffering, there are no good answers that satisfy *why* we suffer. Generic well wishes can feel like salt in a wound. We don't realize how quickly words about God can transform from nice to harmful until we're on the receiving end of someone's failed attempt to make sense

LEARN
ABOUT IT

Theodicy, derived from the Greek words for "God" and "justice," represents the philosophical and theological attempt to reconcile the existence of an all-powerful, all-knowing, and all-good God with the presence of evil and suffering in the world. It grapples with the fundamental question of why a loving God would allow such terrible pain and injustice. Various theodicies offer explanations, ranging from the concept of free will, which posits that human choice necessitates the possibility of evil, to the "soul-making" argument, which suggests that suffering is necessary for moral and spiritual development. Ultimately, theodicy seeks to provide a rational justification for God's actions or inactions in the face of human suffering.

of our tragedy. Worse still are theological assertions that suffering is somehow our fault.

In Jesus and in the Suffering Servant before him, we have examples of what it looks like to face suffering for what it is and, by grace, find within it a path of personal and societal transformation. We would never choose this path or wish it on those we love. But when there is no way out, it's at least comforting, and at times emboldening, to know that those who have walked the path before us were able to speak of it with humility and a gratitude that we cannot understand until we find ourselves in the same place.

⎯⎯

THE REVEREND DR. MARTIN LUTHER KING JR., through his writings and recorded speeches, is a boundless source of political analysis, deep conviction, and spiritual insight. He also embodied redemptive suffering until his untimely and tragic death at age thirty-nine.

King did not appear on the American religious and political landscape in a vacuum, nor was he singularly responsible, as the media often portrays him, for the accomplishments of the civil rights movement. However, he captured the imagination of those who dared to believe that the time had come at last for our nation to reckon with slavery's legacy and the evils of racism.

It helped that the well of King's convictions ran deep. He came from Baptist preachers, and from an early age King's parents instilled in him a strong aversion to segregation, as well as a belief in the hope that the omnipotent, or all-powerful, God could "make a way out of no way"—that because of Christ, God would somehow bring good from the evils inflicted on him and others. This hope in God's redemptive purposes in suffering has sustained Black Christians through historic brutalities like slavery, Jim Crow, lynching, and segregation.

This hope in a God who works to change the world was found in King's early writings, where he drew a clear distinction between passive suffering and suffering freely chosen. The first only perpetuated injustice. Choosing to suffer for a great good was alive with redemptive possibilities. Like **Mahatma Gandhi**, King called on his people to use nonviolent tactics as a way to absorb the blows of violent reactions to their peaceful demands for equal treatment under the law.

King's early optimism was matched by his own capacity and willingness to endure hardship, something he rarely wrote about or spoke of publicly. "Due

LEARN ABOUT IT

Mahatma Gandhi's philosophy of nonviolence—or *ahimsa*—was central to his leadership in the Indian independence movement. He believed that nonviolent resistance, rooted in love and truth (called *satyagraha*), was more powerful than violence. Gandhi advocated for civil disobedience, boycotts, and strikes. His approach emphasized the interconnectedness of all beings and the inherent dignity of every individual, arguing that violence ultimately breeds more violence, whereas nonviolence offered a path toward lasting peace and social transformation.

to my involvement in the struggle for the freedom of my people, I have known very few quiet days," he wrote in striking understatement. He had endured arrest and prison, two bombings of his home, multiple death threats, and a stabbing that almost killed him. More than once, he admitted, the burdens felt too heavy to carry and he considered retreating to a quieter life. "But each time such a temptation appeared," he wrote, "something came to strengthen and sustain my determination. I have learned now that the Master's burden is light precisely when we take his yoke upon us." King knew that he could either react with bitterness or look for ways to transform the suffering into a creative force. Redemptive suffering became not merely a political strategy for King but a way of life.

The early gains of the civil rights movement had always been for King the first step in addressing the greatest of social inequities: poverty and lack of access to education, employment, and safe living conditions. But when he turned his attention to economic issues, many of his admirers seemed genuinely surprised, and these later writings still receive less attention and acclaim than his entreaties for racial equity. Indeed, every choice King made in the final years of his life sparked controversy: the decision to move to Chicago to highlight the perniciousness of racism in the North; his growing focus on issues of poverty and economic discrimination; and, most dramatically, his public opposition to the Vietnam War.

After his anti-war statements, many former allies, most notably

President Lyndon Johnson, severed all ties with him. Crowds still flocked to hear him whenever he spoke, which gave him a national platform, but other liberal allies had also retreated. Still, his continued fame mobilized his detractors, including J. Edgar Hoover, the director of the FBI, who was intent on destroying King. There was also increasing conflict within his inner circle of advisers as they struggled with the practical needs of achieving his vision of a multiracial movement of poor people to descend upon Washington, D.C.

If King had known few quiet days in 1960, by 1967, his life was in a frenzy. The Poor People's Campaign was his last plea for nonviolence in a country that seemed to be spinning out of control. He was consumed with a vision to unite the working poor of all races in a common demand for the restructuring of the United States economy. It was poverty, he believed, that destroyed lives and fueled the racism, despair, and violence that plagued our land. Although in public he remained resolute, privately he struggled with depression, fatigue, and doubt. He began to make plans for his succession, all the while pouring everything he had into what his closest allies feared was a doomed effort.

While attending a ministers' conference in February 1968, King heard about the sanitation workers' strike in Memphis. Another attendee, Pastor Billy Kyles, described how, in a spontaneous act of collective defiance, Black workers rose to protest deadly working conditions and starvation wages. The city government refused to negotiate, and as garbage piled up in the city streets, the populace divided along racial lines. Kyles was the first to suggest that King come to Memphis, but his staff quickly responded that he was too busy organizing the Poor People's Campaign to make the trip.

As the strike dragged on, support in the Black community began to wane. When asked to come to Memphis again, he did not hesitate. Going against the unanimous counsel of his staff, he went, and thousands turned out to hear King speak on what would be the first of three visits to Memphis in the last days of his life.

The energy and sense of unity of the crowd buoyed his spirits. He saw in the sanitation workers' courage and solidarity what he wanted to invoke across the nation—a movement of working people standing with dignity to demand safe working conditions and a living wage. He encouraged the strikers to persevere and urged the Black community to stay away from work and school to pressure the mayor to come to the negotiation table. It was the first time King had ever proposed a **general strike**, yet it was in line with what he was increasingly persuaded would be necessary across the nation.

The one-day work stoppage on

LEARN
ABOUT IT

A general strike is a labor strike involving a significant portion of the total workforce in a particular region or country. Unlike traditional strikes focused on specific workplaces or industries, a general strike aims to disrupt the entire economy and exert broad political pressure.

March 28, 1968, was a complete disaster. Strikers and supporters had gathered early, waiting for King to lead them, but his plane was late and the march had to start without him. When he finally arrived, chaos ensued as hundreds swarmed around him. Exhausted from days of nonstop travel, King was disoriented and unprepared for the crowd's response to his presence. Fearing he would be trampled, his security team quickly ushered him to safety. Meanwhile, violence broke out throughout the city. Protesters threw bottles and rocks, looted shops, and torched cars. Police responded with violence, sending panic through the crowds of peaceful protesters.

The riot had dealt a serious blow to the credibility of their movement. King believed that the failures of March 28 could be transformed with a peaceful rally and new work stoppage on April 8. He believed the civil rights movement would either live or die in Memphis.

In his last speech, King began by imagining aloud what he would say if God gave him the opportunity to choose another century in which to live. His response to God was that he would, in fact, choose the present moment. It was a strange thing to consider at a time of so much suffering, he said, "But I know somehow that only when it is dark enough can you see the stars." He acknowledged the threats he received each day and the uncertainty of what lay ahead. "Like anybody, I would like to live a long life," he added. "Longevity has its place. But I'm not concerned about that now. I just want to do God's will." Like Moses before him, God had brought King to the mountaintop to see the Promised Land. "I may not get there with you," he said. "But I want you to know tonight that we, as a people, will get to the Promised Land! And I'm happy tonight! I'm not fearing any man! Mine eyes have seen the glory of the coming of the Lord!" His final prediction was one of acceptance, even transcendence, of death.

King was assassinated the next day.

The sense of destiny that King's parents instilled in him and the conviction that he lived at a pivotal moment of social transformation sustained him to the end, even when it became obvious that he would not live to see the dream God had placed in his heart. Although often discouraged, King refused to succumb to violence or give up hope. He accepted what he could not change, and thrust all his effort into changing what he could.

KING'S COMPASSION NEVER FAILS TO MOVE ME. On the last Sunday of his life, he spoke of the wrenching poverty across our nation, from the northern ghettos to the rural South. He described seeing hundreds of Black children in Marks, Mississippi, walking the streets barefoot, and families living with rats and roaches in their deteriorating apartments. He confessed that he often found himself crying. And on the stormy night before his assassination, as a way to explain why he had come back to Memphis, King reflected on Jesus's parable of the Good Samaritan. In that timeless story, he reminded his listeners, two religious leaders saw a man mortally wounded and chose to pass him by. Only a man of a despised race, the Samaritan, stopped to help. That man illustrated what King called a "dangerous unselfishness," which is the essence of love.

> *"The first question the Levite and the priest [the two religious leaders] asked when they saw the wounded man was 'If I stop to help this man, what will happen to me?' The Good Samaritan reversed the question. 'If I do not stop to help this man, what will happen to him?'... That is the question before you tonight. Not, 'If I stop to help the sanitation workers, what will happen to me?' But 'If I do not stop to help the sanitation workers, what will happen to them?' That's the question."*

King's question is at the heart of sacrificial love and acceptance. Compassion for another places us in service to something beyond ourselves and helps us become larger inside than the suffering we must endure or choose to endure. King believed that only love had the power to break the cycles of violence and hate, as revealed by Jesus on the cross.

When we choose love in response to what we wish we could change but can't; when we choose love as our response to the world as it is, not as what we wish it were; when we choose love over denial, or anger, or cynicism and withdrawal, we share in God's redeeming of our world. It doesn't make the work any easier, but it gives our efforts a sense of purpose that can carry us through.

Through our imperfect efforts, God's grace shines through us in ways we may never know or fully understand.

Acceptance remains among the hardest things asked of us. The price is always high, but in the face of what we would never choose and cannot change, it provides a way forward. We needn't worry if we don't always get it right. In our willingness to stay engaged, God knows that we're all in. Our capacity to love will grow, and through us, God will work quiet miracles that keep hope alive, even in troubling times.

Our lives are full of unforeseen choices, struggles, and callings. Sometimes we can overcome these obstacles, and sometimes we must make peace with them and their inevitability. Sometimes, like Jesus, we are called into the wilderness or to the cross—to physically and spiritually go to those places that challenge us, test us, break us open, and cause something to die within us. Accepting what we did not choose involves a leap of faith that God is present and at work in ways that we cannot comprehend. Sometimes we feel that presence; oftentimes we don't. This kind of acceptance does not mean giving up; rather it is a courageous choice at a decisive moment to embrace the places we are broken as an integral part of a courageous life.

CHAPTER FIVE

STEPPING UP TO THE PLATE

Who knows? Perhaps you have come to
royal dignity for just such a time as this.
—Esther 4:14

Gregory Boyle is a priest and the founder of Homeboy Industries, the largest gang intervention, rehabilitation, and reentry program in the world. This life-changing ministry had its beginnings in Dolores Mission Church, in the neighborhood with the highest concentration of gang activity in Los Angeles. Boyle served there as parish priest from 1986 to 1992, when young men were both killing and dying at alarming rates. Boyle's first idea was to establish an alternative school for young gang members, and the parish convent where six Belgian nuns lived was the only possible site.

In *Barking to the Choir: The Power of Radical Kinship*, Boyle recounts how he approached the nuns: " 'Hey,' I ask. 'Would you guys mind . . . you know . . . moving out . . . and we could turn the convent into a school for gang members?' They looked at me, then at each other, and said simply, 'Sure.'"

The nuns didn't hesitate. With a single word, they did their part.

Like the nuns who said yes, we make some of our most consequential decisions seemingly on the spot, bypassing conscious or logical thinking. A situation presents itself, and we respond with intuition. Instinct is the defining characteristic in these moments, although we can often see how long we had been preparing for them. Like a baseball player who has been training for months, there's nothing left to do but step up to the plate and swing.

Stepping up to the plate was an image that came to me during the intense pandemic months of late 2020. COVID-19 infections and deaths were rising at an alarming rate, schools and businesses were closed, and leading up to the presidential election, the mood in the country—and certainly in Washington, D.C.—was fraught. During that time, I received an inordinately high number of requests for assistance. The appeals came from both individuals and organizations. Some of the tasks were relatively small and manageable; others required considerable commitments of time and energy. There was an urgency, even desperation, in the asking. I was tired, but we were all tired. No matter how I felt, it was time for me to serve wherever and whenever I could. All of my efforts in that season were away from public view, as the majority of "step up to the plate" moments are.

Earlier that year, however, when President Trump stood outside the historic St. John's Church holding a Bible, I faced a stepping-up moment of greater notoriety than I could ever have anticipated. I had spoken out on matters of equal importance before, including gun violence, immigrant rights, and in protest of the president's racist slurs against the city of Baltimore, all with minimal public reaction apart from the churches I served. **This time was different.** It was as if an electric current were running through the country, connecting us all.

When stepping up to the plate in the public arena, it's impossible to know in advance how our actions will be received. There is always the risk of focusing on the response, as if news and social media attention determines the merit or impact of our actions. Yet the most transformative movements require decades of sustained effort before real change occurs, with many lonely people stepping up long before anyone takes notice. Moreover, fame, when it comes, is short-lived and seductive, tempting us to stay in the spotlight or seek out the next one, when in the end what matters most is what

LEARN ABOUT IT

On Monday, June 1, 2020, at the height of the George Floyd protests in Washington, D.C., law enforcement officers used tear gas and other riot control tactics to clear peaceful protesters from Lafayette Square, so President Donald Trump could walk from the White House to St. John's Episcopal Church for a photo op of Trump holding a Bible in front of a building damaged by graffiti and fire during protests the night before.

we do and how we live when no one is watching. That was certainly the case in the summer of 2020.

Immediately after the news of the president's photo op broke, dozens of faith leaders across the region wanted to gather and collectively denounce President Trump's actions and reclaim the sacred space. The energy coming toward our small church staff felt frenetic, but I understood the desire—they wanted to step up, too. We agreed to organize a press conference the next day at St. John's to issue a condemnation. By Tuesday morning, however, police had blocked off access to the church and demonstrators had spilled over into nearby streets, essentially shutting down that part of the city. On Wednesday, as we attempted to make our way to the podium my staff had set up as close to St. John's as they could get, we were overwhelmed by protesters and dozens of journalists who had staked out their places by the front.

One by one, the religious leaders attempted to speak. Our sound system was terrible, and even standing right next to the podium, I could barely hear what they were saying. Apart from the reporters, no one was paying attention. When it was my turn, I was blinded by the lights in my face, and I couldn't think of a word to say. The spectacle was obviously inconsequential to the demonstrators, many of whom had been physically displaced by the media. Off to the side, I heard a young person say, "Sit down and shut up."

I walked away from the podium and sat down on the street next to him. "We've been in the hot sun all day, and no one has paid us any mind," he said with disgust. "Then you show up, and all the cameras focus on you. When you leave, so will they. But we'll still be here." He was right, of course. I apologized. He shook his head and looked away.

A Black minister who was part of the faith leaders gathering came and stood next to me. In a loud voice that conveyed both compassion and authority, he addressed the demonstrators sitting on the street. He thanked them for their witness, encouraged them to persevere, and spontaneously prayed on their behalf. He then took my hand and pulled me to my feet.

"Our sister is trying to do what's right," he said. "Please treat her with respect."

Most seemed unpersuaded, but one young man turned to me and said, "Don't take it personally. It's been a long, hot day."

"More than a day, I imagine," I replied. He nodded. In the realm of justice, and indeed all of life, stepping up to the plate isn't something we do once, but time and again, when it feels as if the world is watching and, more important, when it's not.

Sometimes when the moment comes, we instantly know that we have the skills and resources needed for a given task, and we embrace it with confidence. At other times, we feel woefully inadequate and unprepared, yet saying no doesn't feel like an option. In those situations, we learn either to trust a power greater than ourselves acting through our offerings, or we learn the hard but necessary lessons of failure. Other times, we hear a call that blissfully lifts us out of lesser concerns to do something brave or good, and our past missteps and present shortcomings don't seem to matter.

Clearly the easiest version of stepping up to the plate is when we feel ready and well equipped to do it. The task may be large or small. It could be something we're excited about or that we dread, but we can accomplish with relative ease what for others would be more difficult, if not impossible. We are functioning from an area of strength.

For example, I read about a small group of scientists at the National Institutes of Health who realized that they were on the verge of a breakthrough in treating a rare form of leukemia. Driven by that prospect, they worked around the clock for weeks, missing their children's soccer games and piano recitals so that someone else might live to see their own children play. Surely that same tenacity helped epidemiologists around the world develop multiple vaccines for COVID-19 in a remarkably short period of time, no doubt at enormous personal sacrifice. Most of us couldn't step up to that particular plate, but they could and did, so that others might live.

I again think of Martin Luther King Jr.'s decision to go to Memphis, a reminder that stepping up to the plate means showing up and offering what we have not because we want to but because it is the *right* thing to do.

I also am reminded of two occasions in the life of Jesus. He had returned to his hometown of Nazareth after considerable time away. As was his custom, Jesus went to the synagogue on the Sabbath. When it was his turn to read aloud from the scriptures, he opened the scroll to the prophet Isaiah:

> *"The Spirit of the Lord is upon me, because he has anointed me to bring good news to the poor. He has sent me to proclaim release to the captives and recovery of sight to the blind, to let the oppressed go free, to proclaim the year of the Lord's favor."*

With calm confidence, Jesus then identified himself as the one anointed by God. He had heard his own vocation affirmed in Isaiah's words.

Jesus was clear, and he was ready.

It didn't matter to him when his own community, after initially speaking highly of him, took offense at his words and turned against him. He simply went on his way, to the work that he was called to do. Near the end of his life, Jesus once again stepped up to his destiny, yet with a decidedly different tone and outcome.

As recounted in the Gospel of John, religious leaders in Jerusalem had arrested Jesus, supposedly for healing on the Sabbath. They wanted to silence him for good because his message threatened their hold on the populace and their risky relationship with occupying forces of the Roman imperial government. Lacking the political authority for executions, they appealed to the Roman official Pontius Pilate, suggesting that Jesus was a political risk for the emperor. Dubious of their claims, Pilate had Jesus brought to him.

"Are you the King of the Jews?" he asked.

Jesus answered, "My kingdom is not from this world. For this I was born, and for this I came into the world, to testify to the truth. Everyone who belongs to the truth listens to my voice."

In a question that haunts all who read it, Pilate asked Jesus, "What is truth?"

Jesus refused to say anything more, choosing not to plead for his life before the puppet ruler of an authoritarian empire. He knew that his time had come to die, and he was ready.

I once knew a man who faced his own death with a Christ-like degree of acceptance that I pray for the grace to emulate when my time comes. His name was Rod Hardy, and his wife, Katie, was the first office administrator I worked with at St. John's in Minneapolis.

The year I was elected bishop, Rod got a diagnosis of cancer. His doctors told him he had a few months left. As Paul and I were getting ready to move to Washington, D.C., we stopped by to say goodbye to Katie and Rod, knowing that we would not see Rod alive again. He greeted us warmly from the hospital bed set up in the family room. Before we could ask him how he was feeling, he peppered us with questions, wanting to know all about the new life awaiting us.

"I can't wait to hear of all your adventures," he said.

We spoke for perhaps twenty minutes. When Rod began to tire, Paul cleared his throat and told him how much he appreciated his friendship and support over the years. We were all silent for a moment. Then Rod spoke up: "I want people to watch me now, because I'm going to die as if everything we say on Sunday in church is true." He smiled. "Go on. You're going to love your new life." When I returned a few months later for Rod's funeral, Katie told me that he had lived his last days with grace and gratitude. Even when stepping up to the plate isn't a matter of life and death, it can embolden us to take a leap of faith, stepping into an arena of influence, offering ourselves in service to others.

Since Bishop Michael Curry's election as the presiding bishop of the Episcopal Church in 2015, he has won love and respect across the world. His sermon for the royal wedding of Prince Harry and Meghan Markle in 2018 inspired the two billion people who heard his message of the power of love.

"We were made by a power of love, and our lives were meant—and are meant—to be lived in that love. That's why we're here," he said. Addressing the young couple, the family gathered to celebrate that love, and everyone looking on from around the globe, Curry invited us all to imagine a world guided by unselfish, sacrificial love, "where no child will go hungry ever again, poverty will become history, and we will lay down our swords and shields and study war no more." As he spoke, we all wanted that kind of world, and to be the kind of people to usher that world into being.

That's Bishop Curry's gift.

How he came to be our presiding bishop, with a global platform for his message of love, is another example of stepping up to the plate. For many years, Curry was a beloved leader of the Episcopal Church, serving first as a parish priest and then as bishop of the Diocese of North Carolina. I knew him as a colleague and mentor, and like many, I admired his dynamic preaching, personal warmth, and unwavering commitment to social justice. Throughout his ministry, he was able to take strong public positions on controversial subjects yet maintain genuinely affectionate relationships with those who disagreed.

Early in my years as bishop, Bishop Curry and I were invited by a mutual friend, Bishop Marc Andrus of California, to lead a preaching retreat for clergy. We spent four days together, and it gave me the rare opportunity to learn as much as I could from my more experienced colleagues. One evening I asked Bishop Curry how he managed to do his work with such joy. He said that he tried to focus his energies on the things he did well, which were preaching, teaching, and spending time with clergy. "I don't really like meetings," he told me. "So I try not to accept invitations that involve a lot of sitting around." He seemed truly content.

A few years later, I watched as Bishop Curry stepped with confidence into the election process for presiding bishop. He spoke with grace, good humor, and authority. He was generous and kind to the other candidates. There was not a trace of arrogance in him, only strength and contagious joy. It was as if he knew that he would be elected to lead a faith community with 1.6 million members, the first Black man to lead a predominantly white church with historical ties to slavery and Jim Crow.

I kept thinking back to our conversation in California, because if there was one thing I knew about the role of presiding bishop, it was that it involved attending a lot of meetings and taking on countless administrative burdens—not the work that he told me he loved best. It was clear that personal preference wasn't what motivated Bishop Curry to seek election as presiding bishop. Nor was ambition, for that matter. He simply heard the call. He knew the work ahead would require personal sacrifice, and still he stepped up.

The bishops eligible to vote in the election didn't talk much about how we would vote, and there wasn't any explicit campaigning among the four candidates. We held our collective breath as we made our way to the church where the election was to take place. I happened to walk alongside Bishop Curry for a short while, and he took my hand.

"For a time such as this, Michael," I said softly, harkening back to the biblical heroine **Esther** at her own iconic moment of stepping up to the plate. He stopped, looked directly at me, and said, "Pray for me, my sister. Pray that I never lose sight of Jesus."

LEARN
ABOUT IT

Esther, a central figure in the biblical book of Esther, is renowned for her courage and moment of "stepping up" that saved the Jewish people from annihilation. An orphan, she was chosen to become queen of Persia by King Ahasuerus. When the king's adviser, Haman, plotted to exterminate the Jews, Esther revealed her Jewish identity to the king at great personal risk. It worked—she successfully persuaded him to thwart Haman's plan.

He knew. And he was ready.

But what happens when we aren't ready to step up? Or when we know we can't do what's needed, but we're being asked to do it anyway? Reading the Bible is encouraging here, for there are countless examples throughout both the Jewish and Christian texts of ordinary human beings called by God to do impossible-seeming things.

Some of my favorite biblical characters politely tell God they are the wrong person for the job. Moses, for example, insists he can't possibly be the one to tell the ruler of Egypt to release the Israelites from slavery because he stutters. Jeremiah informs God that no one would listen to him because he is only a boy. When Isaiah hears God's call, he collapses into shame. "Woe is me," he laments. "I am lost, for I am a man of unclean lips."

In each case, God in effect says, "I know who you are. I know your shortcomings. Step up anyway." There is a similar refrain among Jesus's disciples, most notably Simon Peter, whose answer to Jesus's call is "Go away from me, Lord, for I am a sinful man." But Jesus knows all about Simon Peter, and he is the one Jesus wants by his side. The message throughout scripture is that whenever God—or life itself—asks you to step up to the plate, it's normal to feel both unworthy and unprepared. It also doesn't matter. We are to enter the gap between our current capacity and what's needed anyway. When good things result, we know deep in our bones "that this extraordinary power belongs to God and does not come from us."

Another compelling example is known as the miracle of the loaves and fish. One of the few stories that shows up in all four Gospel accounts, it tells of a time when Jesus and his disciples attempt to take some time away to rest, but thousands of people follow them to their place of seclusion. Jesus sets aside his fatigue and ministers to them. He instructs his disciples to do the same. At the end of that long day, the disciples plead with Jesus to send the crowds home. "This is a deserted place and the hour is now very late," they say. "Send them away so that they may go into the surrounding country and villages and buy something for themselves to eat."

There are two versions of what happens next. In one, Jesus tells the disciples to provide food for the people to eat. But they have only five loaves of bread and two fish. In the second version, a young boy offers his dinner—again, a few loaves and some fish. In both stories, Jesus takes what is offered, asks God's blessing, and gives the food to the disciples to distribute to the crowd. There is enough for thousands to eat their fill, with twelve baskets filled with leftovers. "Gather up the fragments left over," Jesus orders the disciples, "so that nothing may be lost."

I live my entire life inside the miracle of the loaves and fish.

Nearly every sermon I preach feels incomplete and inadequate, but I preach it anyway, praying that Jesus will fill in the gaps. My leadership is often imperfect and insufficient, but I lead to the best of my ability anyway and wait for Jesus to step in. The money I give away is never enough to meet the need, but I give anyway. I hope that, along with others, I might ease people's pain.

The image of a few loaves and some fish feeding a multitude is meant to encourage us all to give what we have when we know it is not enough. For reasons beyond our understanding, God consistently chooses to work through our imperfect, inadequate offerings.

Failure, however, is often a part of stepping up and learning to be brave. Typically, we don't experience miracles, and the consequences of being inadequate and unprepared is there for the world to see. How we respond in the face of failure is one of the most important decisions we then make. If we can learn to accept failure as a part of growth, trusting that such experiences are part of a larger narrative of courage and purpose, we can gather the lessons we need to learn from the pain and move on. The next time it's our turn to step up, we are better prepared, and in retrospect, we see how essential failure is in learning to be brave.

A few years ago, I came across a short essay addressed to young artists written by Ira Glass, the host and executive producer of the radio show and podcast *This American Life*. He begins by acknowledging the initial distance between artistic aspiration and our first stuttering attempts to express it. "For the first couple years that you're making stuff, what you're making isn't so good," he writes. "What you're making is kind of a disappointment to you."

But what the artist does next determines everything:

> *[If] you are just starting out or if you are still in this phase, you gotta know it's normal and the most important thing you can do is do a lot of work. [. . .] It is only by going through a volume of work that you're going to catch up and close that gap. And the work you're making will be as good as your ambitions.*

Stepping up to the plate when you aren't ready is the price of starting. It's what you must do, time and again, when moving toward something important and becoming the person who is able to do or accomplish what is currently beyond your ability. You show up, take your place, step up to the plate, and swing and miss, and miss, and miss—until one day you make contact.

My public missteps have been among the most instructive, albeit painful, lessons in leadership. They have taught me humility. I've learned that facing my critics, taking in what they have to say and owning my mistakes, is not only the best way to ride out the storm but also to grow in maturity.

For example, three years into my role as bishop, I preached a Christmas Eve sermon at Washington National Cathedral that, to put it mildly, did not go well. Christmas Eve is my annual opportunity to share with a wide audience the most life-affirming message of the Christian faith: that God is love, and for love of humankind, God comes to us where we are, as we are. Given the cathedral's location and audience, there is also an expectation to address the wider issues of the day. The stakes feel high every year.

I had done my best to prepare that year, but my offering, as Ira Glass would say, wasn't very good. I had no choice but to preach what I had and pray that it would be one of those times when the Spirit would make up for my lack of inspiration.

It wasn't.

Worse still, I managed to offend several Jewish attendees and their Christian friends with an example I used. Without intending to, I struck a nerve that shot pain through a large section of the Jewish community affiliated with the cathedral. Some were perplexed and hurt. Others were furious. Word spread, and by Christmas morning, my email inbox was filled with expressions of disappointment and outrage. One person went so far as to contact the religion editor of *The Washington Post* to complain about what I had said. I was mortified.

Several friends tried to make me feel better, going so far as to praise the sermon and dismiss the negative reactions. A few took aim at my critics and encouraged me to ignore them. It was tempting to put the blame on those who came at me with such intensity.

In the scheme of things, this was a relatively minor public misstep, and I have made far more spectacular ones since then. But at the time, I was completely undone. Preaching well matters to me, and not only had I disappointed those who were kind enough not to say anything, but I had caused others genuine distress. The barrage of critique was overwhelming, and I was unprepared for the emotional spiral I went down during the next few days.

Dr. Brené Brown's book *Rising Strong: How the Ability to Reset Transforms the Way We Live, Love, Parent, and Lead* fell into my hands in those turbulent days. It was a lifeline—eleven chapters on the pain and humiliation of failing in any realm of life, large or small, and how to recover from it. Brown refers to an image that defined her earlier work, that of an arena in which someone is willing to fail while daring greatly to achieve something. In *Rising Strong*, however, she lingers on the moment when that brave person has collapsed facedown. I couldn't put the book down.

Reading her words felt like a crucible moment, like a high-stakes test: What kind of public leader would I be?

LEARN
ABOUT IT

Brené Brown's "Man in the Arena" concept is drawn from Theodore Roosevelt's speech "Citizenship in a Republic," which emphasizes the importance of vulnerability and courage in engaging with life. Brown suggests that true worth and growth come from being vulnerable and taking risks, even when there's no guarantee of success, and that the only way to avoid criticism is to do nothing, say nothing, and be nothing, which ultimately leads to a life devoid of meaning.

Brown outlines a simple yet challenging process for rising when we fall, or, as I've come to experience it, stepping up again, this time into the moment presented by having previously stepped up and failed.

First there is "reckoning," when we take stock of where we find ourselves, acknowledging the hurt and disorientation of falling, and moving from judgment to curiosity. Next there is the "rumble," where we truly own what has happened and ask the questions that broaden our understanding. Finally, there is the "revolution"—a term Brown uses to convey the kind of bold transformation that can occur in individuals and society when we become the kind of people who are willing to fail for the things that matter, precisely because we know we can rise again.

I decided to send a personal apology to all who had written to me of their hurt and anger and offer to meet. Nearly everyone wrote back, surprised, and appreciative that I had contacted them. Four accepted my invitation, and in the new year, I welcomed each one into my office. I listened to their stories, which helped me better understand why my words had been so offensive. I didn't agree with every point they made, but I was reminded of the power of language to trigger pain. Our differences mattered less than the fact that we were talking about tender issues of faith and identity.

I also discovered that I could step up to the plate of turmoil I had created, and in doing so, defuse a volatile situation. In *Love Is the Way*, Bishop Curry writes about "learning how to stand and kneel at the same time," that is, hold true to his convictions while receiving anger from another person with compassion and respect.

It was critical for me to allow those I had hurt to express their anger, take it in, and remain standing. It is a lesson I must relearn with every failure, both public and private.

I wish I could say that failing gets easier, but it hurts just as much each time. Still, there is no other way I would rather live or lead. That's the revolutionary part, Brown argues: "When the process becomes a practice—a way of engaging the world—there's no doubt that it ignites revolutionary change. It changes us and it changes the people around us."

A third and perhaps the most faith-affirming way we experience the call to step up is when we are feeling stuck in the complexity of our lives. To be called outside of ourselves to do something brave and good in a completely different sphere is sheer grace.

The classic example comes from Jacob, whose story is told in the book of Genesis. A word of warning for those who haven't read the early biblical texts: Much of what we find there is offensive to modern sensibilities. In the ancient world, slavery, polygamy, patriarchy, and violence were treated as normal, and like some in our time, many people, including those writing these texts, believed that such atrocities were God-sanctioned.

Fortunately, there is a corrective thread throughout scripture and an admirable willingness to acknowledge the failures and sins of our spiritual ancestors. In other words, the Bible tells stories of imperfect human beings and their encounters with God through sweeps of history that are as messy as our own time. As

LEARN
ABOUT IT

The biblical story of Jacob and Esau, twin sons of Isaac and Rebekah, is a narrative that explores themes of birthright, deception, and the unfolding of God's purpose. Esau, the elder, is a skilled hunter, while Jacob is described as a quiet man. Their differing personalities and their parents' favoritism create tension. Esau's impulsive decision to trade his birthright to Jacob for a bowl of stew, and Jacob's subsequent deception to obtain his father's blessing, set in motion a complex relationship marked by conflict and eventual reconciliation.

each generation reads the ancient texts through a new lens, they reveal fresh insights that provide meaning, challenge, consolation, and guidance. I am among those who believe that through the texts, God speaks to those who choose to listen.

Back to **Jacob**, who, by all accounts, is a scoundrel and thief. As a young man, he steals his older brother **Esau**'s birthright and then proceeds to cheat Esau out of their father's blessing—a particular ritual of the ancient world that could be bestowed only once. At his mother's urging, Jacob leaves home, seemingly to find a wife among their kinsmen in another region, but equally important, to escape Esau's rage.

Jacob meets his match in his future father-in-law, Laban, himself an opportunist. After a love-at-first-sight encounter with Laban's youngest daughter, Rachel, Jacob asks for Laban's blessing to marry her. Laban agrees, but only if Jacob works for him for seven years. After Jacob completes his side of the arrangement, Laban tricks him into marrying Rachel's older sister, Leah, assuring Joseph that after seven more years' labor, he can marry Rachel as well. Jacob agrees and eventually is married to both daughters. Jacob prospers in his father-in-law's household—so much so that Laban and his sons become suspicious of him and their relationship sours.

Amid this family drama, God speaks to Jacob: "Return to the land of your ancestors and to your kindred, and I will be with you." It is as clear a call as Abraham had received before him, and he, too, answers without hesitation. He conspires with both his wives to plan their escape. They slip away early one morning, taking with them all that they can carry, including the sacred objects in Laban's household.

On his way back to his homeland, Jacob's past returns to haunt him, as he rightfully worries about how Esau will receive him. After sending a peace offering, Jacob hears word that his brother is coming to meet him, accompanied by four hundred men. Now Jacob is truly frightened.

After sending his family ahead for protection, Jacob waits alone for his brother to arrive. Here the story shifts into the mystical. Out of the darkness a stranger appears and attacks him, and they wrestle all night. Jacob seems resigned, but he keeps fighting. At one point, the man strikes Jacob's hip, seriously wounding him, but Jacob does not relent. At sunrise, the stranger pleads with Jacob to let him go. "I will not let you go," Jacob replies, "unless you bless me." "You shall no longer be called Jacob," the stranger says to him, "for you have striven with God and with humans and have prevailed."

We come to realize alongside Jacob that he had been wrestling all night with God. "I have seen God face to face, and yet my life is preserved," he marvels afterward. The blessing he asks for and receives is his alone, supplanting the blessing he stole from his brother. The next day Jacob and Esau meet and reconcile. As an acknowledgment of the blessing's cost, Jacob limps for the rest of his life.

What strikes me here isn't Jacob's deviousness, which remains a constant, but that time and again, God looks past his selfish, deceptive actions and calls him to take his place in the lineage of God's people. He has cheated his father and his brother, yet God's grace and love are greater than his sins and failing.

I've lost count of the times I have been rescued from the downward spiral of my thoughts, anxieties, or foolish actions by the call to step up to something else. That pivot doesn't take away or solve my life's ambiguities and contradictions, but for a time, I'm lifted out of them, free to focus my attention on something worthwhile, to do something for someone else.

———

IN EARLY SEPTEMBER 2021, I felt sadness to the point of despair washing over me. The end of summer is often a time of melancholy for me, and that year it was particularly intense. We had said goodbye to our adult children and young grandchildren, not knowing, given pandemic precautions, when we would be able to see them again. I faced the prospect of returning to work after several weeks away where multiple tasks were waiting, none of which I wanted to do. It was as pure a depressive state as I've experienced in some time, and I was perfectly content to sink further down.

Then I remembered that a neighbor was organizing what she called a "yard giveaway" (as opposed to a yard sale) that weekend to help immigrant families who had been particularly hard hit by the pandemic and subsequent economic shutdown. Feeling weary, I almost let the opportunity to help pass by, but late one night I packed up our car with dishes, pots and pans, blankets, clothes, and furniture. The next morning, I drove to the site of the giveaway, a basketball court near a large apartment complex in a part of the city I had never been to before.

On the basketball court, a dozen or so volunteers were organizing a mountain of donations into what looked like the first floor of a department store while a line formed outside. Children ran around the perimeter, pointing excitedly to the bicycles and toys. When the gate opened, it felt like Christmas morning.

My job was to escort elderly residents as they made their selections. One woman, whom I learned was suffering from cancer, asked me to hold her bag. As we walked through each station, I watched teenage girls try on jackets and pass pairs of jeans between them, seeking the right fit. Younger children held stuffed animals.

Couples carried furniture back to their apartments. As the court emptied of goods and people, I spoke with the women who had organized the event. They were tired and gratified, and already making plans for their next effort.

What I gave away from our household and my presence at the gathering were of modest help that day, but what I received was a priceless gift. Simply being in a community that was practicing love raised me out of my crippling sadness to a space of gratitude. When the giveaway was over, I was still the same person with the same struggles. But joining in the act of hospitality allowed me, for a time, to break free. It was a grace-filled reminder of God, who sees all my brokenness and responds not by simplifying or condoning, but by inviting me to step out of myself and into something worthwhile. Whenever it happens, I am, like Jacob, grateful for God's willingness to work through my imperfections. It's not a matter of being good enough for God or anyone else, but of answering the summons that beckons us forward.

THOSE WHOSE STORIES I'VE BEEN PRIVILEGED TO SHARE in this book all had their "step up to the plate" moments, some of personal significance and others with a societal impact echoing across time. One reason I am captivated by the struggle for racial justice and civil rights in this country is that the historical narrative ties together so many of those courageous moments, as individuals make possible what has long seemed beyond reach and inspire future generations to carry forward the dream. My focus has been primarily on personal stories, but the collective account is equally powerful. For when brave souls come together in common purpose, led by those who helped them believe that their contribution matters, the world changes for the better.

Let's return to the triumphant moment in 1965 when Martin Luther King Jr. spoke from the steps of the state capitol building in Montgomery, Alabama, for it was the hard-won fruit of countless acts of courage. The resistance to voting rights for Black people in Alabama (indeed, for civil rights of any kind) had been fierce and ugly. The journey from Selma to Montgomery began in bloodshed, when, on March 7, marchers had been violently turned back on the Edmund Pettus Bridge. Thanks to the presence of television cameras, the nation witnessed the carnage, and King seized the moment. He wasn't on the bridge during what is now known as Bloody Sunday, but he led a second attempt to cross two days later, defying local edicts outlawing the march. Moreover, he called upon white clergy and people of goodwill from around the country to join him in peaceful protest. Hundreds immediately made their way south, including Washington National Cathedral Dean Francis B. Sayre Jr.

After days of negotiation and local demonstrations, a federal judge granted protection for a limited number of people to make the journey from Selma to Montgomery, and the fifty-four-mile walk began in earnest. At every turn, local authorities and white vigilante groups threatened the marchers with violence. Television cameras and journalists joined the five-day pilgrimage, as did National Guard troops, there to protect the marchers. Thousands of Black men and women from across Alabama risked their lives and their livelihoods to meet King on the road. The power of the march lay in the number of people willing to put their bodies on the line.

One such man was a Black railroad worker named Henry Caffey, who lived in the small town of Trickem, Alabama. Caffey had worked for the railroad all his life, laying, straightening, and repairing sections of track by hand. By 1965, Henry had risen to the rank of section master, the highest position to which a Black man could aspire in his field. He was a respected employee and on good terms with most of the white men for whom he worked. Henry's teenage daughter wanted to join the march as it passed near Trickem.

I learned the story of Henry Caffey and his daughter from my colleague Andrew Waldo, who grew up in Montgomery in the 1960s, the son of an Episcopal priest. As a boy, Andrew had played with the children of civil rights leaders, both Black and white, and he's always been passionately interested in trains and how the railroads shaped our nation's history. Andrew returned to Montgomery as an adult to interview as many of the retired workers of the Western Railway of Alabama as he could find. One afternoon, he sat on Caffey's front porch, listening to the old man reminisce about those turbulent years.

The Selma to Montgomery march was a stepping-up moment of enormous consequence, certainly for the young girl, but also for her father. As they made their way on the three-mile road between their home and the highway, a state trooper recognized Caffey's car and pulled him over. The officer wrote a ticket and said, "Henry, take your daughter back home, and I'll tear up this ticket." Caffey replied, "You can write up as many tickets as you want. My daughter's going to march in that march."

Among the white clergy traveling to join the march was a twenty-five-year-old Episcopal seminary student from Cambridge, Massachusetts, named Jonathan Daniels. Daniels shared the idealistic aspirations of many young Northerners, and he had become awakened to America's harsh racial disparities through an urban ministry internship in Providence, Rhode Island. His decision to go to Selma nonetheless came as a surprise because, earlier that same year, he had publicly defended the Episcopal bishop of Alabama, who had explicitly told Northern Episcopalians to stay out of his jurisdiction.

Daniels was among a group of seminarians who, on March 7, watched the carnage on the Edmund Pettus Bridge on live television. When he heard King's plea for religious leaders to come South, Daniels decided to raise money to help other students make the journey rather than go himself. At that evening's chapel service,

LEARN
ABOUT IT

The Magnificat is a significant passage in the Bible, found in the Gospel of Luke (1:46–55). It expresses Mary's joy and gratitude to God for choosing her to bear Jesus and is rich in theological themes, including God's mercy, care for the lowly, and reversal of worldly power structures.

however, as Daniels joined in singing what's known as **the Magnificat**, or Mary's Song, he had what can only be described as a conversion experience, as the mother of Jesus urged him to go to Selma.

Daniels and his companions were among the two thousand peaceful protesters who marched with Dr. King through downtown Selma, but after they crossed the Edmund Pettus Bridge, they were abruptly stopped by order of a federal court. At this stage in the civil rights movement, King would not defy the federal government, their only real protection against Southern extremism. Many who came to march returned home in disappointment.

Feeling uneasy with such a short and fruitless witness, Daniels and his seminary classmate Judy Upham chose to stay in Selma. Alongside them was the Reverend James Reeb, a Unitarian minister from Boston, who had been on the same flight as Daniels. That evening, Reeb was attacked and killed by white vigilantes as he was leaving a Black restaurant, his death sending a chilling message to everyone who remained: They, too, were risking their lives.

After President Johnson delivered a speech to a joint session of Congress in support of the Voting Rights Bill, King finally secured federal permission and promises of protection. Daniels and Upham were then among the more than three thousand people who walked out of Selma on the first day. From there, only three hundred people were authorized to continue on the narrow highway that led to Montgomery. Daniels helped shuttle people back to Selma, and he returned each night to set up campsites and keep guard. The crowds returned for the final stretch five days later. Daniels and Upham were there on March 25 to hear King's jubilant speech as twenty thousand people stood with him before the state capitol.

As the marchers hurried to leave Montgomery before nightfall, Viola Liuzzo, a thirty-nine-year-old white woman who had driven down from Detroit to participate, was bringing a group of students back to Selma on a desolate stretch of Highway 80 when a car filled with Klansmen sped past her car. One man rolled down his window, aimed a gun, and shot her dead. Stunned by Liuzzo's death, inspired by the courageous witness of so many, and having fallen in love with the Black family who took them into their home, Daniels and Upham stayed in Selma all spring, registering voters and tutoring elementary school students. Daniels also served on a dialogue committee with prominent white leaders in Selma, including members of the local Episcopal church, many of whom were resistant to integration of their congregation.

By then, the national spotlight had left Selma, as King focused his energies elsewhere and racial tensions flared in Northern cities. But Daniels's sense of vocation had been fixed ever since the night he had sung the Magnificat in the chapel. As Stephanie Spellers writes in her book *The Church Cracked Open: Disruption, Decline, and New Hope for Beloved Community*, "Mary's revolutionary cry helped turn Daniels's face toward Selma."

And there he stayed.

Daniels and Upham returned to school for final exams, and by July, Daniels was back in Alabama to devote the entire summer to activism and voter registration, one of only a handful of white civil rights workers in the state. Camera and notebook in hand, he was determined to document the abject poverty and abusive treatment Black residents endured and, in whatever ways he could, improve them. If conditions were poor in Selma, they were even worse in the neighboring Lowndes County, the poorest in the state. There, Black people outnumbered white people four to one, and most worked as sharecroppers on former plantations under conditions not much better than in the days of slavery. Segregation was un-compromisingly cruel. Black residents who tried to vote were re-fused, or subjected to literacy tests, and often fired from their jobs afterward.

Far from the national spotlight, twenty-four-year-old Stokely Carmichael and the Student Nonviolent Coordinating Commit-tee (SNCC) were making slow inroads through painstaking or-ganizing efforts in Lowndes County, and Daniels wanted to be among them. John Lewis, at the time the twenty-five-year-old na-tional chairman of SNCC, would later say of Daniels that he had become like kin to the county's Black farmers and a leader in his own right.

History was made on August 6, when President Johnson signed into law the Voting Rights Act of 1965. Federal voting registrars soon began arriving in Lowndes County. Meanwhile, national attention was fixed on California, where the largest Black rebellion since World War II broke out in the Watts neighborhood of Los Angeles. The mood among white residents in Lowndes County grew more ominous as they feared a similar uprising. In such a charged, paranoid environment, the simple act of registering to vote was considered a threat to white supremacy.

Many Black students, too young to vote yet determined to be heard, stepped up to the plate. Working with SNCC organizers in early August, a group of students planned a protest in the predominantly white town of Fort Deposit, Alabama, where Black customers were often denied service in the local stores or charged significantly higher prices. Local SNCC leaders communicated their fears of Ku Klux Klan retaliation to their headquarters in Atlanta and asked for police protection and press coverage. John Lewis sent a telegram to Governor George Wallace demanding protection for the demonstrators, to no avail.

When the white community heard of the planned protest, they armed themselves as if preparing for war. Around ten in the morning, a few Black adults made their way into town and stood in front of the post office, waiting to register to vote. Meanwhile, the young people planned to begin their demonstration from the Methodist church north of town.

Daniels, along with a Catholic priest named Richard Morrisroe, decided to support the teenagers in their first protest. By now, such stepping up was second nature for Daniels. Those present in Fort Deposit that day remember him as relaxed, seeming to enjoy himself as he marched through town. In groups of eight to ten, Black young people walked up to three offending stores carrying protest signs. They were peaceful and orderly, yet as an armed group of white men approached, the Fort Deposit police arrested all the demonstrators, including Daniels and Morrisroe.

Everyone over the age of eighteen spent six miserable days in jail in the nearby town of Hayneville, as lawyers and activists from across Alabama tried to secure their release. Then, on August 20, without explanation, they were told to leave town immediately. Daniels, Morrisroe, and two other young protesters, Ruby Sales and Joyce Bailey, decided to stop and buy soft drinks in the one store in Hayneville where Black people could shop freely. Unbeknownst to them, a white man named Tom Coleman had received word from the sheriff's office about the released civil rights workers and had driven ahead to the store. As Daniels opened the screen door for Sales to enter, Coleman appeared with his shotgun and yelled for them to leave. In the final stepping-up of his life, Daniels pushed Sales out of the way. Coleman shot him point-blank in the chest.

On the mantel in my office, I have a replica of the stone carving of Jonathan Daniels that can be found in the Human Rights Porch of Washington National Cathedral. People often ask me who he is, and I gladly tell the story of a young man who learned how to be brave. Courage cost him his life, yet it also taught him how to live.

Although our stepping-up moments may seem small by comparison, they have a cumulative effect, and there may be far more at stake every time we choose to step up than we realize. We're never more alive than when we take our turn at the most necessary things, fulfill the deeper purposes of our lives, and know ourselves to be accepted despite our failings and called to do something brave.

CHAPTER SIX

THE INEVITABLE LETDOWN

No good deed goes unpunished.
—*Oscar Wilde*

The Christian season of Lent, which calls us to reflect on and change our lives, is patterned on an intense time of trial and temptation that Jesus experienced immediately after his baptism by John in the Jordan River. The juxtaposition is striking. No sooner does the Spirit of God speak to Jesus as he rises from the waters of baptism, saying, "You are my Son, the Beloved; with you I am well pleased," than **that same Spirit drives him into the wilderness to be tempted by Satan.** In one moment, Jesus is basking in the affirmation

LEARN
ABOUT IT

The temptation of Jesus in the wilderness recounts a period of forty days and nights in the desert, where he is then tempted by Satan. Jesus is challenged to turn stones into bread, throw himself down from the temple to test God's protection, and worship Satan in exchange for worldly power. Jesus resists each temptation by quoting scripture, demonstrating his unwavering devotion to God, and foreshadowing his coming ministry, which would be marked by love, obedience, and sacrifice.

of God; in the next, he is contending with his human frailties in a struggle against the force of evil. If Jesus had any delusions of grandeur, they were dashed in the wilderness.

Such is the emotional whiplash that follows many decisive moments. Although circumstances vary, the inevitable emotional letdown that follows a decisive moment can throw us off course and cause us to question the validity or lasting power of what we had thought to be a transformative experience.

During my last year of seminary, I was struggling with indecision between a more traditional track of study and one with a much greater sense of adventure. The traditional classes would be more demanding academically and would keep me on campus. The more adventuresome option would involve commuting into Washington, D.C., each week and taking my place among others who felt called to the gritty world of urban ministry. I had enough perspective to realize that this wasn't a life-or-death decision. Nonetheless, I was truly stuck.

I went for a swim at the local recreation center with this choice on my mind. As I was doing laps, the proverbial lightbulb I had been praying for turned on. I knew without a doubt that the best decision was to stay on campus, focus on essentials, and enjoy the last weeks at seminary. Relief energized me, and I finished my workout strong and confident. But no sooner had I stepped out of the pool and begun to dry off than all the uncertainty returned, overtaking the confidence I had felt just moments before. The letdown came so quickly that I burst out laughing. Then it dawned on me that I could trust either what had happened in the pool or the rush of doubt that followed. In what felt like an act of faith, I chose to go with my experience in the water. The decision no longer seems significant, but the memory has helped me navigate the same swing of emotion when the stakes have been much higher.

Letdown comes in many forms. After the rush of energy dissipates, the most predictable feeling is emptiness. Life usually snaps back to a normal that can feel dull. Doubt rushes in. For a time, we lose our bearings and are tempted to retreat from the path of courage or, equally dangerous, veer into overconfidence, with a temporary sense of invincibility blinding us to what's up ahead.

The Gospels share a pointed example in an exchange between Jesus and his disciple Simon Peter. As Jesus's ministry is gathering momentum and his fame is rising, he takes those closest to him aside to ponder what it all means.

"Who do the people say that the Son of Man is?" he asks them.

"Some say John the Baptist," they reply, a remarkable statement given that John, the leader of the spiritual movement from which Jesus emerged, had recently been beheaded by King Herod.

"But others Elijah," they continue, referring to an ancient prophet who, in Jewish lore, was thought to return as a forerunner to the Messiah.

"Still others Jeremiah or one of the prophets."

Jesus is obviously stirring hope among the populace and igniting dreams of liberation from the Roman occupation. He then asks, "But who do you say that I am?"

With immediate and astonishing clarity, Simon Peter declares, "You are the Messiah, the Son of the living God."

Deeply moved, Jesus exclaims, "Blessed are you, Simon son of Jonah! For flesh and blood has not revealed this to you, but my Father in heaven. You are Peter [a name derived from the Greek *petra*, meaning "stone"], and on this rock I will build my church." To Simon Peter's astonishment, and surely all the others, Jesus elevated him to a position of leadership.

If only the conversation had ended there. But Jesus continues, swearing the disciples to silence, telling them that he is destined to suffer and die when they enter Jerusalem. Simon Peter protests, "God forbid it, Lord! This must never happen to you." Jesus's rebuke is immediate: "Get behind me, Satan! You are a stumbling block to me, for you are setting your mind not on divine things but on human things." Seconds after hearing Jesus's highest praise, Simon Peter is humiliated in front of his peers.

Like Simon Peter, I have mistakenly assumed, in the afterglow of public praise, that an accomplishment or insight in one realm of my life will carry into others. For example, when I was parish priest in Minneapolis, I became involved in a faith-based community organization known as ISAIAH, a multiracial, nonpartisan coalition dedicated to racial and economic justice in Minnesota. Periodically, the leaders of ISAIAH would invite me to be one of the speakers at a community gathering or the lead organizer of a meeting with elected officials. These efforts required significant preparation and practice, and the events themselves were often thrilling. I loved speaking before a crowd or firmly advocating a position within the halls of political power. On occasion, I was effective enough to garner attention and public acclaim.

Invariably, after a meeting or event in which I played a leading role, another group or community organizer would invite me to speak out on a different issue or take part in another action for which I was not prepared. Basking in my earlier success, I would say yes. Suffice to say, the results were always embarrassing. I would feel humiliated and exposed as the political novice that I was. "Never let mistakes stop you," a community organizer once counseled after he watched me retreat after a disastrous meeting with an elected official. "Learn everything you can from this and carry on."

It's noteworthy that Jesus's rebuke doesn't cause him to change his mind about Simon Peter's future leadership. And although Jesus's words must have stung, Simon Peter remains at his side. This wouldn't be the last time he would fail Jesus. The worst was yet to come. After Jesus is arrested, Simon Peter publicly denies knowing him three times. When Jesus is crucified, Simon Peter and the other male disciples flee in fear, while the women of their group remain at the cross.

In one Gospel account, the men return to their home villages and their old jobs as fishermen, paralyzed with grief. Then one day the resurrected Jesus appears, waiting on the shore for them as they bring in their night catch. Overtaken with emotion, Simon Peter jumps into the water and swims ashore. "Come and have breakfast," Jesus says to them. He then assures Simon Peter that he is not only forgiven but also still called to lead. Simon Peter picks himself up and keeps going.

I suppose that it shouldn't have come as a surprise that I'd experience a public fall from grace while still on the receiving end of effusive public admiration for my stance against President Trump. The esteem certainly wasn't universal, but among the people whose opinion of my work matters to me, my public stature had risen considerably. The praise was both affirming and seductive. I was invited to speak on podcasts and write op-eds for national newspapers. The organizers of the 2020 Democratic National Convention asked me to offer a closing prayer. Organizations around the country invited me to preach or lead seminars. In late January 2021, I was featured in a church publication extolling my leadership.

Then in February 2021, a decision that I made with my colleague, the Very Reverend Randolph Marshall Hollerith, dean of

Washington National Cathedral, prompted such harsh and sustained public critique that for several weeks I wasn't sure if I would remain a bishop.

We were still in the early period of pandemic lockdown, months before vaccinations were available. Washington National Cathedral was enjoying a national wave of public gratitude for its high-quality online worship that provided a spiritual lifeline for thousands of homebound people across the country. The dean had begun inviting prominent clergy from a variety of traditions and theological perspectives to record sermons later aired as part of the cathedral's virtual Sunday worship. Most of the guest speakers were well received. But on the Friday morning before a prominent evangelical Christian preacher and author, Max Lucado, was scheduled to preach, Randy called me, and I knew why.

By then word had spread that Lucado would be speaking from the cathedral's pulpit. It prompted alarm on social media platforms because of statements he had made in the past against LGBTQ+ people. Soon there was an organized effort to persuade Randy and me to rescind the invitation. We both considered ourselves strong allies of LGBTQ+ members of the church and assumed that our solidarity was not in question. In a phrase I have often used in attempting to lead across differences, I thought that "we could afford to be generous" with those who held other views, to create civil discourse on contentious topics.

"Who are you asking to be generous?" one person shot back.

LEARN
ABOUT IT

Matthew Shepard was a college student who was tortured and killed in an anti-gay hate crime in 1998 that helped spark the movement for LGBTQ+ rights. Twenty years after his murder, Matthew's ashes were interred at the Washington National Cathedral and the Right Reverend V. Gene Robinson said, "Gently rest in this place. You are safe now. And Matt, welcome home." Each year for Shepard's birthday, his parents gather with the cathedral community to celebrate him and his legacy, and to advocate for a more just and compassionate world.

"Would you ask Black Christians to be generous in listening to a white supremacist?"

The Dean and I watched Lucado's prerecorded sermon. His topic was on the power of the Holy Spirit in our lives with no mention of his views on human sexuality, and we didn't think it would cause offense. Moreover, Lucado had privately expressed to Dean Hollerith his regret for the insensitivity of the remarks he had made years before. We decided to air his sermon.

The public outcry was overwhelming. For days, my inbox was flooded with hundreds of emails expressing hurt, anger, and confusion. In anguish, people asked why we had ceded the cathedral pulpit, our most esteemed public platform, to someone who refused to renounce the cruel statements he had made and whose church was not a welcoming place for LGBTQ+ people. Some wrote long paragraphs, recounting childhood memories of having Max Lucado's words read to them by their parents and pastors; of being rejected by their congregations when they came out as gay or lesbian; of living in fear for the safety of their transgender children and grandchildren. The letters were heartbreaking. When I tried to express my rationale in a social media post, it only made things worse.

The intensity of the emotions coming toward us—confusion, disappointment, grief, and rage—stopped me cold. LGBTQ+ members of the cathedral congregation asked in disbelief why we hadn't consulted them. The leadership bodies of the diocese wondered the same thing, and many clergy felt personally betrayed. I also caused a pastoral crisis for many in their congregations, they told me, as yet again I had asked those most harmed by the church's bigotry to pay the larger price in the interest of building relationships with evangelical Christians. People across the country demanded to know how we decided, and when, and what the process was for vetting cathedral preachers. Our most vocal critics called into question our commitment to justice, interpreting past decisions in light of this one.

Not all the feedback was critical. Some people wrote to say that we had done the right thing by not bowing to public pressure and that the whole affair was an example of our society's toxic polarity, intolerance, and cancel culture. Their words were intended to reassure us, but they didn't. They may even be true, but the fact remained that I had hurt people I loved and caused many to question whether the Episcopal Church was a safe spiritual home for them. There was nothing I could do except the painstaking work of apology and restitution. Past mistakes had taught me the steps, but knowledge didn't make it easier. For a solid week while I was in quarantine at an Airbnb in Minneapolis (waiting for a clear COVID-19 test so that I might hold our newborn grand-daughter), I rose each day alone and responded to every angry and hurt email. I began tentative dialogues with the critics who were willing to engage. Many were not, but some did graciously, includ-ing the mother of a transgender child who told me that she wor-ried for their life every day and LGBTQ+ colleagues who asked if I thought they would ever be welcome to speak in Max Lucado's church. I had humbling conversations with friends who assured me of their love, but said they needed me to know how much I had hurt them. The presiding bishop was pastorally supportive, but also clear that Randy and I needed to make a public apology, which we did several times. Max Lucado also apologized in writing to us for past statements he had made that had caused so much pain. He did not, however, move away from his church's position against the full acceptance and inclusion of LGBTQ+ people.

But apology wasn't enough, which was evident the evening we held an online dialogue in which several hundred Episcopa-lians from across the country expressed their views on the inci-dent. Dr. Kelly Brown Douglas, the cathedral's canon theologian, acted as facilitator, a generous gesture given how disappointed she was in our actions. Others helped us strategize how to bal-ance the need to listen with the need to answer questions. What we heard underscored how little I understood about the lives of LGBTQ+ people and their families, and how sometimes the worst pain is inflicted upon them by those who imagine, as I did, that we were incapable of such harm. After ninety minutes on Zoom, the event ended without a sense of resolution. The social media conversation continued for days, and as hard as it was being the subject of criticism and speculation, I stayed in it as best I could.

The ordeal was a hard lesson in how quickly I could lose the trust that had taken years to establish and how much work would be required to build it back again. It also was painfully obvious that past actions of courageous leadership granted no immunity from the consequences of a public mistake. Eventually the storm blew over, and I settled back into the more natural state of doing my work without public notice. But for months I had the same feeling that I have after a near accident (or an actual one) when riding my bicycle. Our blind spots are dangerous precisely because we can't see them. On my bike, and in life, I'm particularly vulnerable to a fall when I feel on top of the world.

Letdowns are inevitable, but they do not have the final word unless we let them. Nor do they cancel out the initial gift of motivating insight that seems so far away when the letdown is at its height. Still, it does take time to recover from the disorientation. We need to be honest with ourselves and others when we make a mistake. It's a way of living and leading with an undefended heart, truly open to others, but with a spine strong enough to withstand the experience, learn from it, and carry on.

Sometimes it's the people around us who contribute to the let-down after an experience of courage or clarity. A few of my mentors jokingly called this "payback," and much of it is simply the price of being in a relationship with others. When our sons were young, for example, I came to expect payback from being away for any length of time; the house would be a disaster, the boys cranky, and Paul not particularly interested in hearing what had happened to me while he was tending to things at home. I felt hurt, but they were the ones who bore the brunt of my going, and I needed to allow them their emotions. I recognized the same behavior in myself whenever Paul's work took him away from us.

There are more damaging expressions of payback, however, that cross over into emotional abuse when unequal power dynamics are in play: a parent preventing a child from pursuing her dream that would take her away from the family, a coach holding back a gifted athlete because of his race, partners preventing or sabotaging one another's progress for fear of being left behind, a teacher humiliating a promising student in front of their peers.

In my first job out of seminary, I worked as an assistant priest at Trinity Episcopal Church in Toledo, Ohio, alongside a priest who had a reputation, as my bishop had warned me, "for having trouble working with women." I wasn't sure what that meant, but I was determined to be the exception to that rule. To his credit, that priest hired me when I was nine months pregnant and gave me a position with considerable responsibility and freedom. But he never was comfortable with my success and with the congregation's growing affection for me. I came to expect humiliation whenever I accomplished something of significance or was publicly praised. Payback would come in the form of an insult to my appearance (or overly sexualized praise); a harsh critique of a sermon or something else I had done; or, after he knew my vulnerabilities, a carefully placed comment intended to upset me.

This man could also be encouraging and overtly supportive of my ministry, so these experiences of payback were doubly upsetting. After some time had passed, he would revert to his public stance of affection and praise. Whenever I mustered my courage to speak to him about something hurtful that he had said or done, he claimed ignorance or suggested that I was overreacting. His gaslighting made me feel crazy. I spent three years doubting my perceptions of what was happening and trying to be good enough to please him, without being so good that I overshadowed his oversized ego.

My point here is that what we experience as a letdown or payback—in my case, the push and pull I experienced each time I inadvertently ran afoul of my boss in my achievements—is as much about our relationships with other people as it is about ourselves. Stepping out in courage affects those around us. Even in our most loving relationships, we bear the cost of disruption to the patterns we've come to expect from one another. Decisive moments also can trigger the worst in human behavior, when one person, or group, or indeed the entire society, seeks to undermine or prevent the life-affirming progress of others.

Backlash is the sociological term to describe the harsh, often violent reaction against greater political and civil rights and other measures of social equality for previously marginalized groups. The word came into popular usage in the early 1960s to describe the fierce white opposition to gains made by Black Americans during the civil rights movement.

Journalist and author Ta-Nehisi Coates's essay compilation *We Were Eight Years in Power: An American Tragedy* is a particularly compelling study of white backlash. He draws haunting parallels between Barack Obama's two-term presidency and the post–Civil War Reconstruction Era—both historical moments of exemplary Black leadership that prompted ferocious opposition among white people. The title of *We Were Eight Years in Power* refers to a speech that South Carolina Congressman Thomas Miller gave in 1885 in which he described all the good that had been done during the eight years that Black politicians controlled the legislature during Reconstruction. He pleaded with his white colleagues not to disenfranchise Black citizens, to no avail. Racial discrimination was codified in the new state constitution, as it was throughout the South. Where legal measures failed, they gave way to more violent means to maintain white rule.

Beyond making the obvious case for interpreting the first election of Donald Trump through the lens of backlash to the Obama years, Coates traces the legacy of white supremacy from the Civil War forward and our tendency as a nation to, at shining moments, "reach for the best part of itself, only to quickly retrench to the worst part of itself."

Coates describes himself as someone who would like to believe in God but can't, having learned at a young age that no god would save him from the brutality of this world. Instead, he has found spiritual meaning in his family, work, and ancestry, and in telling Black history that "does not flatter American democracy, but chastens it." I am drawn to Coates's writing for its poetic brilliance and historical narrative, but also because he finds the same call in atheism that I hear as a Christian to pursue the truth no matter where it leads and to live with hope grounded in things as they are.

"I don't ever want to lose sight of how short my time is here," he writes. "I don't ever want to forget that resistance must be its own reward, since resistance, at least within the lifespan of the resistors, almost always fails . . . And if tragedy is to be proven wrong, if there really is hope out there, I think it can only be made manifest by remembering the cost of it being proven right."

We live with the many echoes of societal backlash, yet we simply cannot afford to collapse in despair. "We are all responsible," my colleague the Right Reverend Eugene T. Sutton, bishop of the Episcopal Diocese of Maryland, insists as the Episcopal Church

LEARN ABOUT IT

Reparations is a national reconciliation and apology to descendants of enslaved African Americans in the United States, encompassing U.S. chattel slavery and its legacy through and beyond the Jim Crow era. Reparations can include financial and practical assistance, as well as memorial and other public acknowledgments.

takes up the issue of **reparations** for our complicity in slavery and white supremacy. As we do, we must accept backlash into the equation of our work and persevere. We do not choose where we are in the human story, only how we live in the time we are given.

There are spiritual parallels to the realities of letdown, payback, and backlash. For in every religious tradition, a high price is placed, rightfully so, on mountaintop experiences—those moments that offer perspective and vision for our lives, when we feel what we can only describe as the palpable presence of God, or a sense of the sacred, however we name it.

For some, faith begins with such a moment, often referred to as a conversion experience. It can be a wake-up call of epic proportions, feeling oneself unconditionally loved, rescued from disaster, forgiven for past mistakes, and enabled to start over. For others, their spiritual consciousness has a far less dramatic beginning, with no one defining experience but instead a gradual sense of being led or inspired to live within a certain faith tradition or to open themselves to the mystery of the divine.

Yet much of the spiritual life—as life in general—is lived not on the mountain but in the valley, when the sense of God's presence is far less dramatic—if we sense God's presence at all. The challenge then is to trust that whatever vision or grace that was given to us when we were at highest was real, even when its emotional intensity fades, along with our confidence, as we come down again. Particularly jarring is the first few days after a transformational encounter or experience, when it seemed as if our life was poised to change, only to find ourselves back where we were before it happened. And worse, feeling the pressure to fall into line.

For the past several years, I have sought the counsel of a wise priest, Bill Kelly. He listens to my life's struggles with empathy and kindness and then offers bits of wisdom from the tradition in Roman Catholicism known as **Ignatian spirituality**, named for the sixteenth-century Spanish founder of the Jesuit order, Ignatius of Loyola. Among the most helpful has been St. Ignatius's understanding of the interplay between what he called experiences of spiritual consolation and desolation.

LEARN
ABOUT IT

Ignatian spirituality uses discernment and reflection to help people find God in all things through prayer, meditation, and contemplation. It is marked by engagement with *your* daily life and discovering an awareness of God's presence within it.

As the words imply, spiritual consolation comes to us in moments of intense joy or beauty, feelings of well-being and life purpose, of love or forgiveness. They are all wonderful in themselves, and they also can be the means through which we experience the love of God. Spiritual desolation is the opposite: those times of discouragement, apathy, heartbreak, and suffering that are not only difficult to endure but also cause us to question the reality of what we thought our "spiritual experiences" were and the presence, or very existence, of God.

To be sure, moments of consolation are what make the spiritual life worth living, and St. Ignatius was adamant that they are available to all people, not just a select few enlightened individuals.

Times of desolation or unhappiness are also universal, and from St. Ignatius's perspective, require deeper understanding and exploration than generally offered or discussed among people of faith. Desolation is not merely going through a hard time; it's as if the spiritual lights of our lives go out completely. In a time of desolation, everything that once gave us confidence in God's love and presence collapses. Like other forms of letdown, desolation causes us to doubt the validity of our uplifting and inspired moments of consolation.

The resources available to us in desolation are ones we all recognize: the empathy and solidarity of a good friend, the solace of nature, the small blessings of daily life, and the mercies of rest. Desolation is not a time for life-altering decisions. As hard as it is, this is time, if possible, to persevere in small, life-affirming acts and tend to our souls with gentleness and grace—or just to hang on, in whatever ways we can. St. Ignatius would encourage us to hold close the memory of better times—consolation—and do our best to live as if they were true, even when we have lost confidence in them.

A key insight from Ignatian spirituality is that the feelings associated with both consolation and desolation are instructive, but they are not constant, nor does one reflect reality more than the other. Acknowledging this makes it easier to experience our emotions for what they are, allow them to wash over us, and let them go. We become less impressed by the feelings associated with consolation and less swayed by the feelings of desolation when they overtake us.

Neither consolation nor desolation last forever; each eventually gives way to the other. As the author of the Psalms writes, "Weeping may linger for the night, but joy comes with the morning."

A final example of letdown: For ten years I worked as a conference leader for Episcopal clergy. The goal for every gathering was for participants to come away with renewed vision and clarified goals for their ministries. Our task on the leadership team was to establish optimal conditions for participants to have mountaintop experiences of lasting value, enabling our world-weary colleagues a chance to rest, take stock, and dream boldly once again.

As part of the required reading material for the conference, we gave the attendees an article to read that describes the power of a "big, hairy, audacious goal," known as a BHAG. A BHAG, I would explain, is a clear, compelling catalyst for change that begins a creative process, and a journey marked by courage and the willingness to take risks. Accomplishing a BHAG requires collaboration with others and at least ten years of hard and sustained work. There are no guarantees of success. Yet even naming such a future vision had a powerful effect; we could see it in the participants' eyes as they gave voice to what had been given them. But then we would all go home—back to our real lives, with all their stressors and competing demands.

I would sometimes run into participants later. As if they were case studies in letdown, almost everyone confessed to disappointment in themselves for not being able to fulfill what they had set their sights on. "Don't give up," I would say, as much to myself as to them. "What you experienced and gave voice to when we were together was real. Dare to trust it even when you can't feel it anymore."

I realized that I needed to end our conferences with a frank conversation about reentry and the inevitability of letdown as something to factor in even as we're still on the mountaintop, looking off toward our preferred future. I made it my practice to paraphrase Albert Einstein's definition of genius as 1 percent vision and 99 percent *alignment*.

The work of alignment is never easy, is almost always messy, and may well evoke resistance in those around us and even backlash from the wider society. It will most certainly involve long stretches when nothing much seems to be happening. There will be times of desolation, calling into question everything we experienced on our proverbial mountain. But the journey through the valley is not optional. Moreover, it doesn't get easier, no matter how many times you go through it.

As I was packing up my desk in Minnesota in preparation for our move to Washington, D.C., I found my own plan from one of those conferences, written thirteen years before, in the back of a drawer. I could never have guessed then how my life would unfold, nor how I would understand in a new way what I had once believed about my future and had come to doubt.

"Dare to believe you are called to leadership," I had written.

In the letdown that followed, I not only felt disappointment but also shame. How dare I imagine such a thing? Eventually, the path of preparation and skill-building presented itself, and I had to learn once again how to live and lead in the slow lane.

The valley is where we cultivate, among other things, the virtue of perseverance.

CHAPTER SEVEN

THE HIDDEN VIRTUE OF PERSEVERANCE

And when you get down to it . . .
that's the only purpose grand enough for
a human life.
Not just to love—but to persist in love.
—Sue Monk Kidd

Madeleine Korbel Albright was the first woman to serve as United States Secretary of State. Even a cursory summary of Albright's professional accomplishments could fill pages, yet she begins her memoir, *Madam Secretary: A Memoir*, acknowledging the implausibility of her career. An immigrant from Czechoslovakia, the mother of three children, she was almost forty years old before she held her first position in government. "Well into adulthood, I was never supposed to become what I became," she writes. "But if I had a late start, I also hurried to catch up." Catch up she did, building upon the foundation of an upbringing well suited for international diplomacy.

She was the eldest child of a diplomat who was forced to leave Czechoslovakia with his family twice, first to England when the Nazis invaded in 1939, and again to the United States in 1948 when communists aligned with the Soviet Union took control of the country. By the time she was a teenager, Albright was fluent in Czech, French, and English. As a student at Wellesley College, she aspired to be a journalist. In the years devoted to furthering her husband's career and raising their children, she studied Russian and began work on a PhD.

Alongside her studies, she did the kind of volunteer work expected of women in Washington, D.C.: fundraising, serving on boards, volunteering at polling stations, and hosting international guests. She also liked the day-to-day tasks of motherhood, from sewing costumes to carpooling and helping her daughters sell Girl Scout cookies. Although in retrospect it may look like she always had her sights set on the highest levels of diplomacy and politics, her lived experience was different.

"My life felt like a jigsaw puzzle," she acknowledges, "only I was working with several pieces from several puzzles simultaneously and there was no finished picture to tell me how it should all end up."

Albright died on Wednesday, March 23, 2022, and in preparation for officiating at her funeral at Washington National Cathedral, I spent several weeks reading her memoirs. It felt like taking a master class in life and leadership. At the funeral, then-President Joseph R. Biden and former president Bill Clinton praised her career. Former Secretary of State Hillary Clinton told stories of her brilliance, wit, and style. Her three daughters recalled her fierce love. Albright's memoirs touched upon all these elements of her life, but what struck me most was her perseverance. She did not make light of her struggles; she was aware of both her strengths and her vulnerabilities, and she readily admitted her mistakes.

"Lives are necessarily untidy and uneven," she writes. "It is important, however, to have some guiding star. For me, that star has always been faith in the democratic promise that each person should be able to go as far as his or her talents will allow."

She had worked hard to become, as Senator Barbara Mikulski described her in 1992, a "twenty-five-year overnight success." As with all those whose lives we admire, much of that work was hidden from view: rising at four thirty each morning to work on her dissertation, working for weeks behind the scenes before an event, mastering new languages and the complexities of global politics, and picking herself up after making a costly mistake, losing a political battle, or, most devastating, when her husband asked for a divorce.

In another memoir, *Prague Winter: A Personal Story of Remembrance and War, 1937–1948*, Albright explores the Jewish heritage that her parents kept from her and the cataclysmic events of her childhood, including the deaths of three grandparents in

Nazi concentration camps. She doesn't hesitate to describe these experiences of cruelty, betrayal, and dreadful choices made in desperation, but she also declares, "they are not what I will take with me as I move to life's next chapter. In the world where I choose to live, even the coldest winter must yield to agents of spring and the darkest view of human nature must eventually find room for shafts of light."

She concludes with this:

> [The] goal we see, and the good we hope for, comes not as a final reward but as the hidden companion to our quest. It is not what we find, but the reason we cannot stop looking and striving that tells us why we are here.

Perseverance is what Albright is describing here, and it is the hidden virtue of every courageous life. Rarely do we see or understand what it costs others to do what may seem effortless to us. We also rarely know what it took for them to carry on when they were tired or discouraged or when they had to start again after failure or disappointment. Wherever we find ourselves standing before a decisive moment in our life's trajectory, perseverance is what enables us to keep going, even when we're stumbling in the dark.

Some people have a natural gift for perseverance. I know for certain that I do not, because I've had to learn it. As a child, I would watch my peers do what I believed came easily to them. When I couldn't do the same, I quit. I had modest aptitude in music and sports, but I never excelled in anything because I didn't know how to practice and fail, over and over, until crossing a threshold to a new level of competence.

I managed to get through high school and into a decent college even though I ran away from every academic discipline that intimidated me. In college, I panicked because there was so much that I didn't know how to do. For the first time in my life, I worked hard to keep up with my accomplished classmates—my first attempt at perseverance. But because I had such a poor academic foundation, I worked long hours with little to show for my efforts. It would take me an entire semester to write a ten-page paper.

You could say that I got through college on perseverance alone, if you define perseverance simply as effort. However, now I know that to be too narrow a definition. It wasn't until I began graduate studies in seminary that I learned the rudiments of writing. In my first year, a classmate who would become a lifelong friend, Linda Kaufman, sat me down and taught me the skills that I later watched my own children master in eighth grade. Linda was the first person to explain to me how to approach a body of information, organize my thoughts, write a first draft, and keep revising it. With her help, I wrote four ten-page papers in one semester. It felt like a miracle.

Still, the die was cast and there remain to this day considerable gaps in my knowledge base and weaknesses in my approach to accomplishing a task, academic or otherwise. I've learned how to persevere with intention, but mostly I still lean on the intuitive side of my brain that I've relied on all my life. It's a messy process and takes far longer than the results suggest, but unlike in my childhood and adolescence, I know now to persevere when things are hard.

My formative lessons about perseverance in leadership came with the call to serve as rector of St. John's in Minneapolis. At age thirty-three, I could not believe my good fortune—not merely because I needed to get out of the church in Toledo, but more astonishingly, because St. John's was the church of my dreams, a community filled with energy, joy, and passion for justice. The move to Minneapolis was a leap of faith for our family, particularly for Paul, who had to leave a teaching job he loved.

Then the church of my dreams became the struggle of my waking hours. The members were plucky, strong-willed, and proud of their community focus. Their journey back from near closure to becoming a destination congregation for young adults and families raising children was admirable. But it didn't take long to realize that the infrastructure upon which the life of the community depended was far more fragile than anyone realized. The initiatives that St. John's took the most pride in were sustained by a handful of people. There was conflict among the leadership, the building was in shabby condition, big maintenance issues were looming, and the annual operating budget was tight.

As a result, my leadership would not be defined by the bold, prophetic ministry I had imagined, but rather the largely invisible task of tending to a small and struggling institution. The congregation also did not respond to me in the way I expected. They were proud of their decision to call a woman with two young children as their priest, yet few were ready to allow me to lead. Most of my early suggestions were ignored.

I had a few decisive moments at St. John's in those years, but they were rare. Mostly it was the slow, steady effort of building trust, setting an inviting tone in worship, fixing a leaking roof, recruiting volunteers, trying my best to inspire in the pulpit each week, making mistakes, learning from them, and starting again. In the beginning, it took every bit of effort I had to remain calm and focused when things weren't going as I had hoped.

In this and similar moments, I learned that perseverance in leadership involved rolling up my sleeves and doing the very thing I didn't want to do. As in academics, perseverance in leadership isn't simply a matter of trying hard; there are disciplines, theories, and material to master. I already had some sense of this before I left Toledo. As I navigated my former boss's inappropriate and at times mean-spirited comments in those years, I noticed how his caustic moods and erratic behavior reverberated through the entire congregation, even among those untouched by his more egregious acts. It dawned on me that overall damage to the community was worse than his behavior toward me, for it was being held hostage by his poor leadership, and like a family with an alcoholic parent, he had inordinate control over its emotional sense of well-being.

LEARN
ABOUT IT

Rabbi Edwin Friedman (1932–1996) was known for his work in family therapy and leadership. His work is known for applying family systems theory—or the idea that a family is composed of unique, interrelated parts that affect one another and the whole—to leadership in faith communities and beyond.

At the suggestion of a friend, I read a book on congregational leadership by **Rabbi Edwin Friedman** titled *Generation to Generation: Family Process in Church and Synagogue*. It was revelatory. In the second chapter I came upon a passage describing the adverse effects of secrecy that took my breath away. He begins, "Family secrets act as the plaque in the arteries of communication." Then talks about how family secrets keep some people apart and others together when they should not, about how secrets distort and confuse us because we see an incomplete picture, and finally how secrets make every problem in our lives worse because they "function to keep anxiety at high levels."

Friedman was describing my church in Toledo. I didn't know what our secrets were, but evidence of them was everywhere. I also knew that I needed help. I mustered up my courage and called Friedman to ask if I could join one of his seminars for clergy. He wasn't receptive, as groups had already been formed, and he suggested that I apply for the following year. I pressed harder: "Is there any way I might start sooner?" He was quiet for a moment and then asked, sounding slightly irritated, "Have you read my book?"

"I'm reading it now," I replied.

"Do you understand it?"

"Yes," I lied. A month later, I found myself traveling to Bethesda, Maryland, on a journey I would take twice a year for the next decade.

Rabbi Friedman taught me a theoretical framework for building a healthy, fruitful, and integrated leader. He argued that this wasn't merely an appealing way for us to live but essential to the health of our whole community, because an organization can rise only to the health and maturity of the people who lead it.

In Minneapolis, I did my best to live and lead by the principles that Friedman taught. He and his team helped me learn to deal with conflict directly or indirectly, depending on the situation. They encouraged me to lead transparently, acknowledging what I didn't know without ever faking weakness to make others feel more powerful. They gave me practical tools to lower anxiety, deal with resistance, and learn from those who disagreed with me. I failed as often as I succeeded, but in failure as much as in success, I learned how to persevere.

Friedman also believed that an essential characteristic of leadership is having a spirit of adventure. The safest place for ships is the harbor, he'd say, but that's not what ships are for. Equally critical is persistence. Still another characteristic is resilience. As the saying goes, he would remind us with a smile, no good deed goes unpunished.

When I received word of Friedman's premature death in 1996,

I sobbed in Paul's arms. How would I continue without him as a ballast in my life? Soon afterward, however, I had a sensation that I can describe only as a blessing, as if Friedman's spirit was assuring me that if I remained a student of leadership, I would be fine.

Friedman was always quick to say that leadership skills are beneficial for everyone, from parents to presidents, because they allow us to handle well the authority entrusted to us and create environments where others can thrive. These are the building blocks of sound relationships and a democratic society. Improving our capacity to lead, wherever we find ourselves, is a lifelong quest. With open hearts and minds, we can learn from anyone, and everyone around us benefits when we embrace the leadership that is ours.

During this time, I had become involved with a group of leaders in the Diocese of Minnesota who wanted to address the sharp decline in membership and participation in all our congregations. Together we began to study the models of leadership in the fast-growing evangelical churches in Minnesota and across the country. I attended seminars led by prominent evangelical Christian leaders, and from them I learned compelling strategies to bring back to my own church. I was welcomed warmly by those whom I assumed, given our opposing positions on social issues, would have nothing but disdain for someone like me. Their teaching led me to other sources, both religious and secular, and a course of study on congregational leadership that culminated in my Doctor of Ministry degree in 2008.

One theory has greatly informed my understanding of how to

lead a community through a sweeping change—the ultimate test in perseverance. In sociology, the theory is called the "diffusion of innovations."

Diffusion-of-innovation theory explains how and why large groups of people come to accept new ideas—and whether they'll accept them quickly or slowly. It offers both a strategy for engagement and a means to overcome the natural human resistance to change. Through many studies, the idea of diffusion became understood as a complex process in which an innovation is communicated over time among members of a group or organization and gradually adopted by those members in stages.

Although seemingly straightforward, the process is rarely smooth and almost always fiercely resisted at first. Later, however, when the innovation has become the norm, the group forgets that initial resistance, particularly those members who fought hard to prevent its adoption! The outcome is never certain, but when systemic change occurs, it is because all the steps in the process of change have been taken.

There is also a mystical, spiritual dimension to crossing the threshold of change that for leaders of faith like me feels like the power of the Holy Spirit. For when we reach what the apostle Paul called the "acceptable time," or what Greek philosophers referred to as *kairos*, or "opportune time," things happen easily and rapidly, and in retrospect, inevitably. Such moments, however, are built on countless other moments of invisible work.

Learning diffusion-of-innovation theory was both a valida-
tion of my early experience and a game changer for my leadership.
It makes such sense, and provides a road map for guiding a community through the process of change, whether it's a small church
launching a big fundraiser, the Diocese of Washington develop-
ing a planning process for coming to terms with its racist past, or
American society, as we grapple with the overwhelming realities
before us, such as gun violence and climate change.

It isn't enough to be right, or even to keep doing the same
things repeatedly and expect things to transform. Hope, as they
say, is not a strategy. Leadership requires the slow, steady work of
building power through relationships and positioning ourselves to
be most effective when the threshold moments come.

There is also a heart component to perseverance, which Jesus
emphasized when teaching his disciples about prayer. He did so
by telling stories, such as one about a man who kept pounding on
the door of a friend's house in the middle of the night demanding bread, and a widow who incessantly hounded a judge for the
justice she deserved. These characters were hardly saints, as if to
underscore the fact that there is nothing visibly admirable about
perseverance; they display only grit and dogged effort. According
to the Gospel of Luke, Jesus told these parables to encourage his
disciples to pray continually and not to lose heart. He knew that
life can be hard and disappointments are real. Like Jesus's first disciples, we're bound to feel discouraged, and perseverance is what

enables us to keep going until we find our footing again, so that we might connect to our heart energy and draw strength from it, even when there may be little to show for our efforts.

Yet simply trying hard doesn't serve us any better in prayer than in the rest of our lives, if it isn't balanced by a commitment to mindfulness and a willingness to learn some basic skills. Without them, perseverance in prayer can run amok, leading us down the path of magical thinking and the confusion of our desires with God's. We fall prey, in the words of Peter Gomes, "to a false and phony version of the Christian faith that suggests that by our faith or our prayers we will be spared the burdens of life."

Perseverance in prayer, then, isn't just about doing it more, but allowing our hearts to be stretched by the trials and struggles of life so that our capacity for love and forgiveness grows, as well as what we are willing to endure for the sake of love.

In a sermon Gomes preached at Harvard titled "Outer Turmoil, Inner Strength," he told the story of Ernest Gordon, for many years the chaplain at Princeton University and, more famously, the author of a memoir of his three-year captivity in a Japanese prison camp that was made into two films, *The Bridge on the River Kwai* and *To End All Wars*. Gomes recounted how Gordon and his fellow captives were initially very religious, "reading their Bibles, praying, singing hymns, witnessing and testifying to their faith, and hoping and expecting that God would reward them and fortify them for their faith by freeing them or at least mitigating their captivity." Their suffering dragged on interminably, more among them died, and God did not deliver them as they had prayed. The men became understandably disillusioned and angry. They abandoned all their outward displays of piety and no longer expected God to save them.

But something else shifted for some of the men as they responded to the needs of their fellow prisoners, as they cared for and protected them and witnessed others sacrificing their lives in love. Quietly they began to speak about the presence of God in their midst. "This was not a revival of religion in the conventional sense," Gomes observed, "but rather the discovery that faith was not what you believed but what you did for others when it seemed you could do nothing at all." Faith returned to them as the result of their compassion, and as they leaned into faith that God was with them in suffering, their capacity for compassion grew.

I wonder if God needs us to persevere in prayer simply because most of what we pray for will take a long time to realize. We pray for healing for ourselves and those we love, knowing that in most cases the process is slow. We pray for peace within our families or in the human family, and we know that peace isn't readily attained and often comes at a dreadfully high price. We pray for justice, knowing that it is always hard-won and takes generations to accomplish.

Remember American theologian Reinhold Niebuhr's words that I quoted in chapter 4: "God, grant me the serenity to accept the things I cannot change, the courage to change the things I can, and the wisdom to know the difference." Niebuhr himself was an extraordinarily persevering man. His generation of clergy began their ministries in the turbulent 1920s, struggling for workers' rights in an age of pervasive greed and disregard for the poor. He lived through the Great Depression, and he spoke against world complacency in the face of Hitler's rise to power. He persisted in writing, teaching, and preaching through the 1960s, when a series of strokes weakened him. He was one of the most influential theologians of the mid-twentieth century, and yet he lived long enough to see his influence wane.

His daughter, Elisabeth Sifton, in a book honoring her father and his associates, writes: "They had both high spirits and serious, dedicated hearts. They worked so hard. They were so very loving. And their labors were informed, in the end, by the humble recognition that it is not within our human powers to understand the final tally." She concludes with my favorite Niebuhr quote, another call to perseverance:

> *Nothing worth doing can be achieved in a lifetime; therefore we must be saved by hope. Nothing that is true or beautiful or good makes complete sense in any immediate context of history; therefore we must be saved by faith. Nothing that we do, however virtuous, can be accomplished alone; therefore we are saved by love.*

We may know that our most decisive moments are preceded by countless small decisions, invisible to others. Yet it's easy to

LEARN
ABOUT IT

Rachel Held Evans was a popular Christian author and religious commentator. She was known for her progressive Christian perspectives, as well as a deep willingness to engage in open and honest discussions about faith, doubt, and the complexities of what it means to be a Christian in modern times.

lose sight of that knowledge as we slog through those stretches of preparation, trial and error, skill-building, and character formation. Perseverance is what keeps us going in the days without drama.

In her last book before her untimely death at age thirty-seven, **Rachel Held Evans** argued against the tendency in Christian theology to focus on Jesus's sacrificial death as if it was the sole purpose of life, reducing the Gospel to a transaction for the world's sins:

Jesus didn't just "come to die." Jesus came to live—to teach, to heal, to tell stories, to turn over tables, to touch people who weren't supposed to be touched and eat with people who weren't supposed to be eaten with. To break bread, to pour wine, to wash feet, to face temptation, to tick off the authorities, to fulfill Scripture, to announce the start of a brand-new kingdom, to show us what that kingdom is like, to show us what God is like, to love his enemies to the point of death at their hand, and to beat death by rising from the grave.

We, like Jesus, are called to take up our cross daily. Or, put slightly differently, we are called to see our acts of daily faithfulness and perseverance as a part of a larger arc of courage and resilience through which the power and the grace of God are at work. The stories we tell and the moments we remember may be about the decisive moments, but what matters most is we *live* these stories each day.

It reminds me of a final story from Rachel Naomi Remen. When she was five years old, she lived with her parents in a small apartment in New York City. Her grandfather would often visit, bearing gifts.

One day he brought her a small paper cup. She looked inside, hoping to find something sweet to eat, but all the cup contained was dirt. Her grandfather smiled at her disappointed face, brought her into the kitchen, and put the paper cup on the window ledge. "If you promise to put a little bit of water in the cup every day, something special may happen," he said. It made no sense to her, but she promised her grandfather that she would, and she did.

At first, she wrote, it was easy to tend to this daily chore, because she was curious to see what would happen. But as days went by and nothing changed, remembering was harder. When her grandfather returned a week later, she asked if it was time to stop. He said no. By the second week, she felt angry and frustrated. When her grandfather came to visit, she wanted to give back the cup. But he refused to take it: "Every day, Rachel, a bit of water." By the third week, she often didn't think of her cup until she was in bed at night. Out of respect for her grandfather, she would get up and tend to her chore.

One morning, there were two little green leaves sprouting up from the dirt that had not been there the day before. She was astonished. Day by day, the plants grew a bit bigger. She couldn't wait to show her grandfather, whom she thought would be as amazed as she was. Instead, he explained to her that life is everywhere, and blessings are everywhere, hidden in the most ordinary and unlikely places.

"And all it needs is water, Grandpa?" Rachel asked.

"No," he said. "All it needs is your faithfulness."

To persevere in faithfulness is our greatest gift to this world. The most influential moments in our lives and in human history depend far more than we realize on our faithfulness in small things, as we rise each day, like Rachel, and put a little water in our cup.

EPILOGUE

*The brave man is not he who does not
feel afraid, but he who conquers that
fear.*   —*Nelson Mandela*

I have learned to expect that when I am at the supermarket, a church
event, or just walking in my neighborhood, people will approach
me wanting to talk about the day President Donald Trump held a
Bible outside St. John's Church or when I gave a homily at the National Cathedral asking the new president to be merciful. Whenever
I am introduced at a public occasion, my responses to his actions
are mentioned, as if they were the most important events in my ordained ministry. In these pages, Reverend Bryan Bliss and I have
sought to place the events of June 1, 2020, and January 21, 2025,
within a larger context, exploring how we learn to be brave over the
course of a lifetime, and in all aspects of life, especially when the
courageous decisions we make are known only to God.

Now in my seventh decade, I think a lot about how to speak
of the challenges of our time with honesty but not despair, with
a sober assessment of the problems we face, and still with genuine hope for our future as a nation and a species. It isn't easy, for

the divisions in our country have only deepened since President Trump left office in January 2021 and then was reelected in 2024. Meanwhile, on the global stage, there are wars in many lands, large-scale migration on nearly every continent, and an ecological crisis imperiling the future of all humankind.

What I keep coming back to, as a source of hope and strength, are the historical accounts of men and women who faced the challenges of their times with grit and grace, the timeless stories of our spiritual and literary traditions that embody courage for us all, the people in my life whose courage and sacrificial love I admire, and the moments I have felt summoned to do what felt impossible at the time. Sometimes I succeeded; often I failed. But what seems to matter most in those moments is that we show up, step up, and make our offering despite its limitations and our own.

I'm equally inspired by the rising generation of leaders to whom the future belongs. Driving to church one Sunday morning, I caught the end of a podcast conversation between Krista Tippett, host of *On Being*, and Ayana Elizabeth Johnson, a marine biologist dedicated to addressing the global climate crisis. Johnson is the editor of an anthology titled *All We Can Save: Truth, Courage, and Solutions for the Climate Crisis*; cocreator of the podcast *How to Save a Planet*; and cofounder of the All We Can Save Project.

From the sound of these titles, you might surmise that Johnson is a naturally hopeful person, but she describes herself more as one drawn to solutions and getting things done. "I'm not a fan of hope as a guiding principle, because it assumes that the outcome will be good, which is not a given," she said. "But I am completely enamored with the amount of possibility that's available to us."

My heart leapt when Johnson spoke of the possibility of our getting things right, that we already have much of what we need to address climate change and other environmental concerns. "We just have to do it," she said. I found myself wondering, in how many other areas of life is it also true that we already have the solutions we need at our fingertips?

Johnson's rejection of a simplistic hope based on wishful thinking is, in fact, very close to the Christian understanding of what hope is—the capacity to face reality, no matter how difficult, and still seek whatever good is possible. As a person of faith, I dare to trust that God is at work amid the most challenging realities of our lives, and that by grace and acceptance, we join God in the holy work of transforming the world. Although I know that God cannot spare us from the consequences of our actions, I hold on to the promise that God will be with us always, to the end of the age. Moreover, I believe that God summons us to work together.

"This is a moment that calls for many leaders," Johnson said, "because what we need is transformation in every community, in every sector of the economy, in every ecosystem, with the hundreds of solutions we have. It's all about how we build a future that we want to live in, where there's a place for us and the people and the things that we love."

In every realm of life, in every country of the world, there are people who choose to be actively engaged to create the future Johnson believes is still possible. They are inspiring to be around because they are themselves inspired and motivated by love. But they are not in a class by themselves—we, too, can join them, and in fact we do, far more than we realize.

I wrote this book to honor the breadth and depth of what courage looks like in decisive moments, whether we are called upon to start, to go out and step up in public, or to stay put and persevere. All require great courage. In the words of the poet David Whyte:

> *Courage is the measure of our heartfelt participation with life, with another, with a community, a work, a future. To be courageous is not necessarily to go anywhere or do anything except to make conscious those things we already feel deeply and then to live through the unending vulnerabilities of those consequences. To be courageous is to stay close to the way we are made.*

My prayer is that, by grace, we all will be emboldened to lean into the wisdom, strength, power, and grace that come to us, whenever we find ourselves at a decisive moment. May you and I dare to believe that we are where we are meant to be when that moment comes, doing the work that is ours to do, fully present to our lives.

For it is in this work that we learn to be brave.

ACKNOWLEDGMENTS

I begin with deep gratitude to Andrew Karre at Dutton Books for seeing in my original work *How We Learn to Be Brave* the potential for a book for young readers. And to wondrous Bryan Bliss, who adapted, refined, and reworked the original into a new creation. This book would not exist without them, and it has been a joy to collaborate with them both.

I also thank Jennifer Gates of Aevitas Creative Management for her steady support, and her unwavering belief in my work.

My vocation as a writer lives within my calling to serve as bishop of the Episcopal Diocese of Washington and Washington National Cathedral, a ministry I share with an extraordinary team of dedicated leaders in their own right. Much of what I get credit for is the result of their work. Special thanks to my assistant, the Rev. Annemarie Quigley, who makes the difficult seem easy. Her brilliance, wide-ranging skills, kindness, and wicked sense of humor keeps us all going on the harder days.

Nothing I do would be possible without the love and support of Paul Budde, my husband of nearly forty years. He is the first and best critic of my writing, and the one who greets me each morning with a kiss and encouraging word as I endeavor to put words on a page.

We first learn what it feels like to be brave when we are young, when nearly every day we must do something that we've never done before. Watching our sons, Amos and Patrick Budde, as they navigated the many brave decisions of their young lives was a master class in courage and Paul and I marvel at the men they have become. Now we are witnessing the same courage in our grandchildren, Lewis and Francine Grantier. They are my inspiration and my joy.

Mariann Edgar Budde

June 4, 2025

NOTES

21   "the most personal is the most universal . . .": Henri Nouwen, *Bread for the Journey: A Daybook of Wisdom and Faith* (New York: HarperOne, 2006), entry for February 23.

29   Author Bruce Feiler describes . . . : Bruce Feiler, *Life Is in the Transitions: Mastering Change at Any Age* (New York: Penguin Press, 2020).

30   "Now the Lord said to Abram . . .": Genesis 12:1–14

30   Sarah laughs. . . . : Genesis 18:12

31   "Heroes have a thousand faces . . .": Joseph Campbell, *The Hero with a Thousand Faces*, 18.

33   "Born in 1899, Thurman . . .": Howard Thurman, *With Head and Heart: The Autobiography of Howard Thurman* (San Diego: Harcourt Brace & Company, 1979), 20.

34   "It may be through the Negroes . . .": Peter Eisenstadt, *Against the Hounds of Hell: A Life of Howard Thurman* (Charlottesville: University of Virginia Press, 2021), 7.

34   While on a sightseeing visit . . . : Ibid., 21.

35   "There are risks involved . . .": Ibid., 207–8.

40   "Lean into it . . .": Anne Tyler, *Saint Maybe* (New York: Alfred A. Knopf, 1991), 213.

43   It is the time you have spent . . .": Antoine de Saint-Exupéry, *The Little Prince* (New York: Harcourt, Brace & World, 1971), 77–87.

43   "If I were called upon to state . . .": Frederick Buechner, *Listening to Your Life: Daily Meditations with Frederick Buechner* (New York: HarperCollins, 1992), 1.

44   "like trees planted by streams . . .": Psalm 1:3

45   "It may be the neighborhood . . .": Joan Chittister, *The Rule of St. Benedict: Insight for the Ages* (Chestnut Ridge, New York: Crossroad Publishing Company, 1992).

46   "Lord, to whom would we go . . .": John 6:60–68

48   "How could a White Jesus . . .": Kelly Brown Douglas, "How Do We Know Black Lives Matter to God?" The Christian Century, September 30, 2020, https://www.christiancentury.org/article/how-my-mind-has-changed/how-do-we-know-black-lives-matter-god.

49   "When I read Cone's words . . .": Ibid.

50   I have always been fascinated . . . : Kati Marton, *Hidden Power: Presidential Marriages That Shaped Our Recent History* (New York: Pantheon Books, 2001), Chapter 2, 74, Kindle.

51   "The bottom dropped out . . .": Doris Kearns Goodwin, *No Ordinary Time: Franklin and Eleanor Roosevelt: The Home Front in World War II* (New York: Simon & Schuster, 1994), 19.

52   "As Eleanor waited . . .": Blanche Wiesen
      Cook, *Eleanor: Volume One, 1884–1933*
      (New York: Penguin Books, 1992), 250.

53   By the time Franklin was elected . . . : 21.
      Marton, *Hidden Power,* 894.

53   In 1944, she was the keynote . . . :
      Thurman, *With Head and Heart,* 141.

55   "I did have a realization . . .": Chris
      Heath, "How Daniel Radcliffe Outran
      Harry Potter," *The Atlantic*, April 30,
      2024.

57   "A journey of a thousand miles . . .":
      Chinese proverb ascribed to Laozi,
      Chapter 64, Dao De Jing.

58   "This is my Son . . .": Luke 9:35.

66   "Sweet Darkness": David Whyte, "Sweet
      Darkness," from *The House of Belonging*
      (1997) and *Essentials* (2020). Reprinted
      with permission from Many Rivers
      Press, Langley, Washington, https://
      davidwhyte.com.

70   "If you get a life . . .": Oliver Allen, "Chief
      Counsel for Equality," *Life* (June 13,
      1955).

72   "confrontation by typewriter . . .":
      Pauli Murray, *Song in a Weary Throat:
      An American Pilgrimage* (New York:
      Liveright Publishing, 2012), 124.

73   "The racial factor . . .": Ibid., 237.

73   "Murray's classmates and professors . . .":
      Rosalind Rosenberg, *Jane Crow: The
      Life of Pauli Murray* (New York: Oxford
      University Press, 2017), 187.

81   "Grant us wisdom . . .": "God of Grace
      and God of Glory," Hymn #584, *The
      Hymnal 1982* (New York: Church
      Publishing, 1982).

82   In an exchange that has inspired . . . : J.
      R. R. Tolkien, *The Lord of the Rings: The
      Fellowship of the Ring, Second Edition*
      (Boston: Houghton Mifflin, 1954), 50.

84   "I will have no right to participate . . .":
      Dietrich Bonhoeffer, Gesammelte Schriften
      [Collected Writings], ed. Ebhard Bethge,
      I:320 (Munich: Haiser, 1958).

84   "No one person is responsible . . .":
      Quoted in *Strange Glory: A Life of
      Dietrich Bonhoeffer* by Charles Marsh
      (New York: Alfred A. Knopf, 2014),
      342, Kindle.

86   "thorn in the flesh . . .": 2 Corinthians
      12:8–10.

89   "As a physician, I have accompanied . . .":
      Rachel Naomi Remen, MD, *My
      Grandfather's Blessings: Stories of
      Strength, Refuge, and Belonging* (New
      York: Riverhead Books, 2000), 29.

90   "Father, if it be possible . . .": Matthew
      26:39.

92   "Yet it was the will of the Lord . . .":
      Isaiah 53:10–11.

93   "Jesus did not simply die . . .": Rachel
      Held Evans, *Inspired: Slaying Dragons,
      Walking on Water, and Loving the Bible
      Again* (Nashville: Thomas Nelson,
      2018), 155, Kindle.

96   "But each time such . . .": James M.
      Washington, ed., *A Testament of Hope:
      The Essential Writings and Speeches of
      Martin Luther King, Jr.* (San Francisco:
      HarperSanFrancisco, 1986), 40.

97   While attending a ministers' conference
      in February 1968 . . . : Joseph
      Rosenbloom, *Redemption: Martin
      Luther King's Last 31 Hours* (Boston:
      Beacon Press, 2018), 32.

99   "But I know somehow that only
      when it is dark enough . . .": James M.
      Washington, ed., *A Testament of Hope:
      The Essential Writings and Speeches of
      Martin Luther King, Jr.* (San Francisco:
      HarperSanFrancisco, 1986), 286.

100   He confessed that . . . : James M.
      Washington, ed., *A Testament of Hope:
      The Essential Writings and Speeches of
      Martin Luther King, Jr.* (San Francisco:
      HarperSanFrancisco, 1986), 272–273.

101   "The first question the Levite . . .":
      James M. Washington, ed., *A Testament
      of Hope: The Essential Writings and*

Speeches of Martin Luther King, Jr. (San Francisco: HarperSanFrancisco, 1986), 285.

103 "'Hey,' I ask. 'Would...'": Gregory Boyle, *Barking to the Choir: The Power of Radical Kinship* (New York: Simon & Schuster, 2017), 29, Kindle.

109 "The Spirit of the Lord is upon me...": Luke 4:18–19.

110 "Are you the King of the Jews...": John 18:28–38.

111 "We were made by a power...": Michael Curry, *The Power of Love: Sermons, Reflections, and Wisdom to Uplift and Inspire* (New York: Avery, 2018), 8–11.

114 "Woe is me...": Luke 5:8.

115 When good things result...: 2 Corinthians 4:7.

115 "This is a deserted place...": Mark 6:36.

117 "[If] you are just starting out...": James Clear, "What Every Successful Person Knows, But Never Says," James Clear, December 14, 2015, https://jamesclear.com/ira-glass-failure.

120 First there is "reckoning"...: Brené Brown, *Rising Strong: How the Ability to Reset Transforms the Way We Live, Love, Parent, and Lead* (New York: Random House, 2017), loc. 202, 274, Kindle.

120 In *Love Is the Way*...: Curry, *Love Is the Way*, 181.

121 "When the process becomes...": Brown, 3605, Kindle.

123 "Return to the land of...": Genesis 31:3.

123 "I will not let you go...": Genesis 32:26–28.

129 The officer wrote a ticket and...: I tell Henry Caffey's story with Andrew Waldo's permission. I first heard Andrew tell the story in a sermon he preached on April 23, 2004.

129 His decision to go to Selma...: Charles W. Eagles, *Outside Agitator: Jon Daniels and the Civil Rights Movement in Alabama* (Tuscaloosa: University of Alabama Press, 2000), 28.

129 At that evening's chapel service...: Quoted in Eagles, 27.

131 One man rolled down...: Rich Wallace and Sandra Neil Wallace, *Blood Brother: Jonathan Daniels and His Sacrifice for Civil Rights* (Calkins Creek, 2016), 137, Kindle.

132 As Stephanie Spellers writes...: Stephanie Spellers, *The Church Cracked Open: Disruption, Decline, and New Hope for Beloved Community* (New York: Church Publishing, 2022), 81.

132 John Lewis, at the time...: Wallace and Wallace, 225.

133 John Lewis sent a telegram...: Eagles, 168.

137 "You are my Son, the Beloved...": 2. Mark 1:11–12.

139 "Who do the people say...": Matthew 16:13–23.

142 Simon Peter picks...: John 21:15–19.

142 In late January 2021...: David Paulsen, "Q& A: Washington Bishop Mariann Budde says Church Should 'Lead with Jesus' in Its Nonpartisan Advocacy," Episcopal News Service, February 4, 2021, https://www.episcopalnewsservice.org/2021/02/04/qa-washington-bishop-mariann-budde-says-churchs-nonpartisan-advocacy-should-lead-with-jesus/.

150 Journalist and author Ta-Nehisi Coates's essay compilation...: Ta-Nehisi Coates, *We Were Eight Years in Power: An American Tragedy* (New York: One World, 2017), 64.

151 Coates describes himself...: Coates, 109.

155 "Weeping may linger...": Psalm 30:5.

155 As part of the required reading...: Jim Collins and Jerry I. Porras,

"Building Your Company's Vision," Harvard Business Review, https://hbr.org/1996/09/building-your-companys-vision. Accessed August 17, 2022.

159 "And when you get down to it . . .": Sue Monk Kidd, *The Secret Life of Bees* (New York: Viking, 2020), 289.

159 "But if I had a late start . . .": Madeleine Albright, *Madam Secretary: A Memoir* (New York: HarperCollins, 2003), 6.

160 "My life felt like . . .": Albright, *Madam Secretary*, 89.

161 "It is important, however . . .": Albright, *Madam Secretary*, 10.

161 She had worked hard to become . . . : Albright, *Madam Secretary*, 6.

161 In another memoir, *Prague Winter* . . . : Madeleine Albright, *Prague Winter: A Personal Story of Remembrance and War, 1937–1948* (New York: HarperCollins, 2013), 414.

162 "[The] goal we see . . .": Albright, *Prague Winter*, 414.

166 "Family secrets act . . .": Edwin H. Friedman, *Generation to Generation: Family Process in Church and Synagogue* (New York: Guilford Press, 1985), 52.

167 "Friedman also believed . . .": Friedman, *Generation to Generation*, 188.

169 Diffusion-of-innovation theory explains . . . : Everett M. Rogers, *Diffusion of Innovations* (New York: Free Press, 1995), 5.

171 We fall prey . . . : Rogers, 169.

171 Gomes recounted how Gordon . . . : Rogers, 11.

172 "This was not a revival of religion . . .": Rogers, 300.

172 "God, grant me . . .": American theologian Reinhold Niebuhr reportedly wrote the prayer in 1932–1933. See Elizabeth Sifton, *The Serenity Prayer: Faith and Politics in Times of Peace and War* (New York: W. W. Norton & Company, 2003), 289.

173 "They had both high spirits . . .": Elisabeth Sifton, *The Serenity Prayer: Faith and Politics in Times of Peace and War* (New York: W. W. Norton & Company, 2003), 348.

173 "Nothing worth doing can be achieved . . .": Sifton, 349.

174 "In her last book before her untimely . . .": Rachel Held Evans, *Inspired: Slaying Giants, Walking on Water, and Loving the Bible Again* (Nashville: Thomas Nelson Books, 2018), 148.

175 It reminds me of a final story from Rachel Naomi Remen . . . : Remen, *My Grandfather's Blessings*, 1–2.

177 "The brave man is not . . .": Nelson Mandela, *Long Walk to Freedom: The Autobiography of Nelson Mandela* (Boston: Little, Brown, 1994), 622.

178 "I'm not a fan of hope as a guiding principle . . .": Anya Elizabeth Johnson, June 9, 2022, https://onbeing.org/programs/ayana-elizabeth-johnson-what-if-we-get-this-right/.

179 "This is a moment that calls . . .": Johnson.

180 "Courage is the measure . . .": David Whyte, *Consolations: The Solace, Nourishment and Underlying Meaning of Everyday Words* (Langley, Washington: Many Rivers Press, 2015), 224 .